Unlocking the Power of Words

Applying the Seven Keys in the PARTNER Model to Create Authentic Conversations

SHYVONNE BALLOSINGH WILLIAMS

CMD GROUP

Unlocking the Power of Words: Applying the Seven Keys in the PARTNER Model to Create Authentic Conversations © 2011 by Shyvonne Williams, CMD Group.

All rights reserved. No part of this book may be reproduced or transmitted in any form or by any means without written permission of the author.

Images contributed by James and Scheyere Moir

ISBN: 978-0-9848198-0-5

PARTNER Invitation

You are hereby invited to PARTNER with me on this book. You can offer your feedback by visiting the web site www.partner-cmd.com and sharing:

- What works well for you and why.
- What you would like to see improved and how.

By PARTNERing together, we will make this book even more effective.

Thank You,
Shyvonne Williams

DEDICATION

I would like to take this opportunity to thank everyone who has supported, loved, appreciated, and encouraged me. I truly believe that I am able to live and thrive because of the love and care surrounding me. I am eternally grateful for every single person in my life—you are all blessings. Because of your love, understanding, caring, forgiveness, motivation, and inspiration, I am able to write.

As the list of people for whom I am grateful is so extensive, I have chosen not to include all the names. Instead, I want to make a promise: I commit to appreciating you and showing you love and gratitude whenever our paths cross. Please recognize that I love and value each of you. Just knowing that you are there for me gives me strength. Thank you for the love and care that keeps me moving forward.

God

Family

CONTENTS

Preface	1
Introduction	5
Key One: Picture	15
Key Two: Articulate	43
Key Three: Realize	61
Key Four: Test	91
Key Five: Nugget	113
Key Six: Evaluate	131
Key Seven: Reinforce	151
Conclusion: The Seven Partner Keys	157
Optional Hidden Bonus Key Eight: Span	167
Glossary	175
About The Author	177
Index	179
Answer Key	182

PREFACE

Before you begin the PARTNER journey, take a moment and visualize yourself sitting by a fire, snuggled up and comfortable, a tasty beverage in your hand. Now, imagine having a chat with someone you delight in, a person with whom you choose to share meaningfully. During the conversation, you listen and learn from one another—you can feel the benefits of this partnership and realize this simple, but profound, chat carries far-reaching, positive effects on your life.

A similar experience awaits you here.

As you read, think of the interaction as a dialogue, an exchange of information powerful enough to enhance your conversations, improve the quality of your relationships, and ultimately bestow greater harmony in your life. This guide is filled with information that has been drawn from my professional background as a life skills coach, mediator, trainer, and group facilitator. It is an interactive learning experience, focused on helping you build bridges of authentic communication.

While reading, you will encounter a variety of concepts. These concepts introduce, and help you to understand, the transformative power of the PARTNER experience. Take note, as you journey through this book, you will find words which have been repurposed to communicate specific ideas. These repurposed words help cultivate your PARTNER skills. When you come across a word with a repurposed meaning, remain open. Breathe in, focus your mind on understanding and accepting the word's new use in the context of a PARTNER conversation. Read the repurposed meaning out loud so you can hear it, write it down so you can experience it, and highlight it so you can see it. Then, apply this fresh meaning as you interact with the material.

In addition to the PARTNER concepts and vocabulary taught in this book, each chapter contains helpful practice exercises that follow the reading sections. These practice exercises offer tools you can use to develop, yourself, your communication skills and, your relationships—they will help enhance your learning experience. These PARTNER "Skill Builders" provide an opportunity to incorporate the practical ideas and concepts of the PARTNER method into your everyday life, and will facilitate your ability to apply the concepts in real time.

If you are nervous about applying the PARTNER keys, let me put your mind at ease. This book takes a gentle approach. Think of it like learning to swim—you begin in the shallow end of the pool, then, with the help of your swim instructor, your ability increases until one day you find yourself swimming confidently in the deep end. The PARTNER Skill Builders function in the same manner as a swim instructor does—they support you until you gain proficiency. The exercises increase your understanding and expand your PARTNERing ability; they help build your skills, equipping you with the tools needed to empower those most important in your life. As you engage in doing the practice exercises you will find yourself swimming comfortably in the deep end, with the ability to PARTNER, without realizing it.

You bring new life to the material, your understanding, your conversations, and your relationships as you use the skill builders and practice what you read. To **REAP** the most benefit from this book:

Read about the concepts.
Execute by doing the skill building exercises.
Achieve competency through repeated practice.
Progress by being a reflective partner.

As you read about the concepts, do the skill building exercises, practice and reflect, you will find yourself building stronger relationships with people. This is but one reward of PARTNERing—increased connection with self and others. You will find yourself inspired to accept others as they are, while at the same time working to improve your personal self. You can best REAP the benefits of PARTNERing through *reflection*. A reflective PARTNER seeks improvement by taking time to learn from experience, contemplating PARTNER interactions, and then determining ways to advance through self-examination and introspection. As you reflect, development occurs and your ability to meet others where they are is improved.

We can experience the beauty and fullness of life when we free ourselves to live in harmony by learning how to accept those around us. My intention with this book is to show how to do just that—simply, easily and joyfully. Will you be my PARTNER? Turn the page to join me now on this wonderful and fulfilling journey…

INTRODUCTION

Welcome to the PARTNER process. As you read about the model, practice the skills, and use the PARTNER keys, you will find yourself letting go of your preconceptions, biases, and barriers to creating stronger relationships. This means that over time you relinquish the urge to tell others how to live. Instead, you help to facilitate their decision making process, freeing them to choose their own path, even if you have objections or fears about their choices. You will not only discover *how* to facilitate and clue into these choices, but also, that you can *empower* others to lead their own lives.

By PARTNERing, you engage in a new kind of dialogue, one where you learn to breathe with tranquility—no matter what the topic of conversation—because, you release your biases and preconceptions. Over time you hear your conversations change, and feel your relationships strengthen, as you become more aware of, and are able to clue into, the other person's perspective. Ultimately you find life tastes sweeter because you see yourself and others, differently and more fully. The flexibility in your relationships increases, creativity rises, and there is enhanced sincerity as you PARTNER. Your conversations touch those around you in new ways, and you begin to emerge as a supportive figure in their lives.

PARTNERing is a process, a method, and an approach. As a process, PARTNERing is a self-transformative tool that will guide you in your own personal evolution. As a method, it is a series of distinctive steps and lessons you can learn to follow in order to deepen your relationships with others. As an approach, PARTNERing provides you with the helpful spirit that will aid you in approaching any kind of dialogue—be it with your colleagues, children, or spouse.

When you apply the PARTNER keys to your conversations, problems and challenges naturally turn into relationship building blocks. PARTNER conversations are guided by the following principle: *clue into and use the other person's perspective as the launching pad for building rapport.* With this premise in mind, you engage in PARTNERing by having people identify the problem from *their viewpoint*, and then support them by continuing to unlock information using the PARTNER keys.

Applying the seven PARTNER keys enhances your ability to uncover the driving force(s) behind any action by tapping into the Unmet need(s) behind the behavior. Once the Unmet need is uncovered, it is used as a stepping stone for creating possibility. This is all done from a place of acceptance. *Acceptance means that you see the other person as whole, complete, and capable.* As part of the PARTNER process you highlight the strengths within the other person. Once identified, these strengths are used to find options that address the unmet needs. Choosing the path of acceptance leads you to authentic relationships where you are able to accept the people in your life just the way they are.

PARTNERing can be used in a variety of personal and professional contexts, and you can conduct PARTNER conversations verbally or in writing. In fact, PARTNERing can be done in person, over the phone, through e-mails, in notes or with handwritten letters. However your PARTNER conversations occur, they facilitate the flow of information and lead to improved connections with the people in your life. Take a moment and think about the relationships you have in your life.

Are you the parent of a teen who is trying to break free? The PARTNER approach nourishes you and your teen's relationship. It opens the doors of understanding, moving you both past conflict to collaboration. By using PARTNER conversations to engage your teen, you spur their willingness to invite you into their lives. When you are aware of what is driving your teen's behavior, you can relate to and support him or her from a place of acceptance.

Are you a manager? Then the PARTNER approach is perfect for you! Think about that employee you just cannot seem to understand. You've tried everything but the two of you cannot see eye to eye. By PARTNERing with that person, you clue into and understand the hurdles he or she faces. You enhance your ability to manage by guiding employees to use their own internal strengths to solve problems themselves. In other words, whether you are talking to your husband, wife, sweetheart, sister, brother, or friend, the PARTNER approach enhances your ability to connect.

The PARTNER philosophy can be incorporated into your daily life and your daily way of being. It is a creed that you can live by. It just takes practice. Remember, the PARTNER model can be practiced through the "Skill Builders"—exercises which are designed to help strengthen your ability to PARTNER. Here is one example of the self-study Skill Builders found throughout the book. Remember to have fun while you do them—think of them as your personal instructor/trainer helping you to sculpt and strengthen your PARTNER muscles!

SKILL BUILDER

Take a moment and in the balloon to the right of the hand list all the things that get in your way of releasing others to make their own choices and decide their own path:

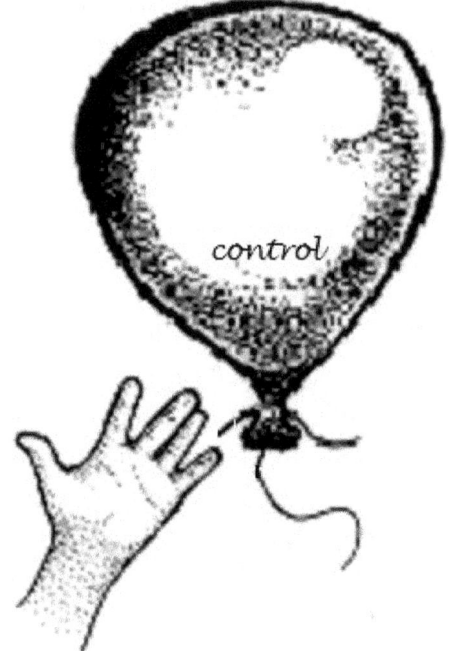

- _____
- _____
- _____
- _____

Once you are done, breathe in with composure. Then, visualize yourself letting go of the balloon and releasing everything inside it. As it rises, feel the weight being lifted from you, hear the inner peace and taste the freedom that comes with release. In the picture draw your expression as you watch the balloon float away and say goodbye.

Since the Skill Building exercises are such an integral part of PARTNERing, feel free to write in this book, or highlight passages that are especially meaningful to you. Make notes in the margins, and fold over the corner on any pages that you find particularly valuable. *This book is your resource.* As you read this material, take time to reflect and practice. It's helpful to venture slowly, go back and review if necessary. As you journey through the keys take time to reward yourself for your progress and, most of all- be open.

The PARTNER model is a special gift. Use it, grow with it, and above all, enjoy it!

WHAT IS PARTNERing?

There are seven *keys* for unlocking the transformative potential of PARTNER conversations:

P *Picture*: unlocks observations

A *Articulate*: unlocks words

R *Realize*: unlocks barriers

T *Test*: unlocks the unmet need or unspoken desire behind the barrier

N *Nugget*: unlocks possible options

E *Evaluate*: unlocks next steps

R *Reinforce*: unlocks feedback and empowerment

Each of these seven keys can be used independently, or they can be used in sequence. Since the PARTNER model is designed to work in a variety of contexts, you are free to use the elements most suited to your needs. For example, the first four keys (PART) help cultivate a *stronger* connection with your loved one, colleague, family member or friend. On the other hand, when problem-solving tools are needed the last three keys (NER) can be added.

The skills integrated into the PARTNER model represent talents that you have needed to use at some time in your life. In fact, you have probably used a PARTNER key within the last week, month or even 24 hours. For example, when you wake up in the morning, you may apply *Picturing*. You may become aware that, although you are awake, you still feel tired, or perhaps energized and ready to go. You look outside and notice that it is raining. While looking out the window you verbally *Articulate* your observation about the weather to your kids. You may use your observation to assess possible barriers by asking the kids if they have coats or rain boots on. You may also observe that the rain causes more traffic and *Realize* that increased traffic can be a barrier to getting to work and school on time.

Once you are aware that traffic can cause a problem you may *Test* to find what is most urgent this morning. As you think about the needs for the morning you may find that your underlying priority is getting the kids to school on time—they have to be there by 8 a.m.! You may then *Nugget* for options: you can drop the kids off and call in to work, you can hurry the kids so they can catch the early bus, or you can follow the normal routine and hope to be on time. You *Evaluate* your options and make a decision: to hurry the kids up so that they can catch the earlier bus. As you're heading out the door, you *Reinforce* and offer feedback as you thank the kids for making the extra effort to get out the door earlier than usual.

As you can see from the example, you already go through your day unconsciously applying different keys in the PARTNER model. Whether you are Nuggeting by generating options for meeting a deadline, Picturing by observing team morale, or Realizing by assessing a barrier to production, throughout your day you already use PARTNER techniques in one form or another. To increase your confidence keep this in mind—believe in yourself. Know that as you read, practice and work with this guide, you will learn to put your skills together in a structured manner.

Another central teaching of the PARTNER method involves increasing your awareness of your own influence. Moving through your day, you can greatly impact those around you. This means your actions, words, and attitudes have an effect on other people. The PARTNER approach teaches you how to use your influence for beneficial results. You can use your influence in one of two ways. First, *positively*—through inspiring collaboration and giving support to the person you are engaging. Second, *negatively*—through pressuring and by coercing others. Each style can be broken down in the following ways:

1. Positively, as a PLUS:

    Produce inspiration

    Lend support

    Unearth knowledge

    Show collaboration

2. Negatively, to PICK:

    Place pressure

    Impose manipulation

    Coerce cohesion

    Knavishly oblige

The important thing to remember is that you are a person of influence. As such, you GIVE by:

Generating thinking in others

Inspiring motivation

Valuing differences

Exhibiting flexibility

To help you visualize this concept, imagine yourself standing beside the person you are PARTNERing with. When your influence is a PLUS, it's like you're standing there with a bag of gifts. However, when you PICK, you're holding an empty bag. What you give is up to you.

The following Skill Builder connects you with the impact of your actions; it will help you identify how to GIVE by *positively influencing* the person you are in dialogue with. In addition, this Skill Builder helps you to uncover the gifts you already have. Once you have identified some of your gifts, you will do some further exercises to help you with strengthening them.

SKILL BUILDER

First, take a moment to visualize what another person experiences when you use your influence to PICK versus using your influence to GIVE. Imagine the expression of the individual as he or she receives a full bag (using your influence to GIVE) or empty bag (using your influence to PICK). Circle what the full bad and cross out the empty container.

Next, recognize that you have an influence on those around you, and proceed with the following steps:

1. Say to yourself: "I will positively use my influence to GIVE, by filling my bag with the following gifts and exhibiting the following traits":

    • <u>Patience</u>   • <u>Appreciation</u>

2. What other traits will you fill your bag with and give to others as you exhibit being a positive influence?

    • _____   • _____

    • _____   • _____

3. Look at the traits you listed and choose one that you want to pull out of the bag. For the next week, think of this trait as a crown that you wear, exhibiting it for all to see. The trait that I commit to exhibiting for the next week is:

4. I know that after a week of focused effort on this trait my skill level will improve. My current skill level in displaying this trait is:

Novice   Pro
1   2   3   4   5   6   7   8   9   10

5. One way to increase your skill level half a step during the next week is to draw a crown on a piece of paper and write the trait you have chosen to exhibit in the crown. Then put the piece of paper in your briefcase, lunch box, near your toothbrush, or on the dashboard of your car—someplace where you will see it and be reminded of your commitment, daily. This is one strategy you can use to increase your skill level. Choose something you feel you can commit to doing and write it below.

6. In a week, I will increase my skill level a half step by:

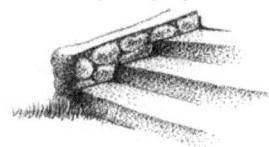

Key One: Picture

You have probably heard the saying "Every journey begins with a single step." In the PARTNER method, that journey begins with *Picturing*. When engaging in Picturing the goal is twofold: first, to *observe*, second, to be *neutral*. When you observe you *gather information*. When you are neutral you gather information *without adding your biases*. Biases get added when your perspective, assessment, point of view, or interpretation distort what you see and hear.

When you Picture, you are an observer. You gather data through your senses - what you see and hear. Observers learn to become very aware of their surroundings; they are present and focused in the here and now. To be an observer requires sharpening your observation skills so you can effectively gather data, intake information, and absorb facts. As you learn about, and enhance your ability to Picture, you begin to *observe neutrally*. You may even find that you begin to observe events as if they were being recorded by a camera. When the camera is *on* you are *observing neutrally*. This helps you to become more fully aware of what another person is trying to communicate.

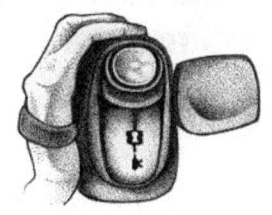

Let's apply the first lesson of Picturing in a brief exercise.

SKILL BUILDER: 1

Picturing is a skill that you can learn with practice. Below is an exercise to help sharpen your skill in this area.

1) Think about a recent interaction you had with another person that did not go well. In the space below describe the event; pour everything out onto the paper below.

_____
_____
_____
_____
_____
_____

2) Think about the same incident and create a time line of the events as they occurred. Focus on the facts.

_____
_____
_____
_____
_____
_____

3) Notes, Thoughts, and Observations. In the space below, write about the difference between 1 and 2. Where were your biases added? What made you stray from the facts? Looking back, what would have helped with sticking to the facts?

_____
_____
_____
_____
_____
_____

EMANATION

Part of absorbing information involves taking in the Emanations of others. *Emanations are actions, behaviors, or moods.* Emanations have two primary roles: first, they are a clue to signal, alert, and draw attention, and second, they communicate a specific message.

As an observer, you observe both *verbal and non-verbal emanations* (signals). Verbal and non-verbal emanations communicate a person's state of mind. Verbal emanations are communicated when the other person exclaims phrases that include, but are not limited to, things like: "Yippee!" or "Oh no!". They are also communicated in other ways, such as when a person lets a sigh out or exhales loudly. In addition to paying attention to people's verbal emanations, it is equally important to observe their non-verbal, physical expressions. A person's body movements and/or facial expressions represent their non-verbal emanations, and are often expressed through: smiles, frowns, or when a person holds their head up high or they hang it down. Paying close attention to both verbal and non-verbal emanations is an essential skill to master, as you learn how to Picture.

When you Picture a situation, keep your observation skills focused on noticing the signals sent by the other person. If you get distracted by interpreting a message from a person's signals, take a deep breath, then, bring your focus back to observation only. Again, try to be neutral, refrain from allowing your biases to cloud what you observe. Refrain from interpretation. To help with neutrality it is useful to understand how biases are added.

Biases are added in a very subtle, unconscious manner as your brain processes information. As you intake information, the brain tries to make sense of what you observe—it tries to fit the observed information into a schema (pattern). To do this, the mind uses past experiences to filter (sort/arrange) the information it receives. In other words, your brain incorporates your perspective, adding it to the observation so that it can interpret the incoming information.

Your perspective is created by your life experience and it helps your brain to make meaning of the world. Your brain is *always* engaged in interpretation. Your goal, as you PARTNER, is to pull out the other person's perspective and understand events from their point of view, instead of projecting your perspective and thereby adding your own biases.

The unconscious process of interpretation is a natural part of human cognition and, on many occasions can be very constructive and helpful. For example, if you observe an out of control car speeding towards you, then your brain's unconscious filtering and use of interpretation is very constructive. In this case your brain fits the observation of an out of control car into a schema. Your brain applies your perspective and finds that based on previous schemas (patterns) there is possible danger. This interpretation tells your body to react and quickly move out of the car's way. In this case your brain's natural filtering to make sense of the information is constructive and protects you. However, when you PARTNER this unconscious process can be unhelpful. Those quick interpretations can get in the way of truly understanding what another person is trying to communicate.

When you PARTNER, the goal is to remain attentive to your brain's unconscious use of interpretation—always remaining mindful of the other person's perspective. This requires observing others, and observing yourself at the same time. Observing self and others helps you to be in tune with how your brain is unconsciously adding to what is Pictured. When bias is added to an observation, the brain strays away from the facts and confuses your perspective for observation. As a conversation PARTNER you want to remember to Picture thoughtfully, instead of reacting impulsively.

Picturing is about *self-observation* just as much as it is about observing others. When you apply Picturing, you observe yourself while at the same time observing the signal(s) the other person is sending without projecting your own feelings onto the other person (e.g., you may want to express blame or judgment during a PARTNER conversation, your Picturing skills will help to resist such temptations).

You can improve your self-observation skill with a little practice. To help you along, try the following skill builder exercises.

SKILL BUILDER: 2

Take a moment and in the space below journal about a time when making a quick interpretation about another was destructive and caused you to miss another person's perspective.

_____
_____
_____
_____
_____
_____
_____
_____
_____
_____
_____
_____
_____
_____
_____
_____
_____

SKILL BUILDER: 3

When I catch myself making interpretations and I want to activate my Picturing skills, I find it helpful to visualize the other person with an open or blank caption. This reminds me to Picture (observe neutrally) and not fill in the blank caption with my interpretation.

There are other strategies that can help with Picturing. Choose something you feel you can use when you notice your interpretations and write your strategy below.

_____
_____
_____
_____
_____
_____
_____
_____
_____
_____

SOS EMANATION

SOS Emanations can appear as *verbal or non-verbal actions, reactions, behaviors, or moods.* Although SOS Emanations may look like attacks, they function as requests asking you, as the receiver, to notice that something deeper is going on. Picturing develops your capacity to observe when an SOS Emanation is being transmitted. Think of them as clues and use your Picturing skills to observe them neutrally.

When Picturing an SOS Emanation, it is important to distinguish between the *signal* and the *message*. Observing the signal means that you stay fact based, focus on the words or actions, not on your interpretation. This can be difficult especially when the other person camouflages the message as a criticism, layers the truth with complaints, understates their uncertainties or evades the emotional effect by projecting onto something else. In reality, though, SOS Emanations indicate a request of some sort, but the request is sent disguised as something else.

For this reason, Emanations of this type may be mistaken for an attack, but when the other person sends you an SOS Emanation it is really a request for you to **clue** into what they are feeling. The SOS-Emanation is really an expression of the other person's concerns. They are sending you the SOS Emanation and requesting that you notice their uneasiness or exasperations. Below are some common examples of SOS Emanations and the method by which they are sent.

C*oncerns camouflaged as criticisms or complaints.* When this occurs the other person shields their concern beneath a complaint or a criticism. Complaints and criticisms hide the request. A complaint is a signal—it is a clue to what the other person feels concern over. When you Picture, observe this SOS Emanation (i.e., *the actual words being used*) without bias. Bias can result in an inaccurate interpretation leading you to react by defending yourself.

L*oss layered beneath labels.* When someone feels loss they can shield this with labels. Labels are accusatory statements. The label "Unsupportive," for example, may be a SOS Emanation rather than an attack on your character; it could be the other persons request for you to notice they are missing you. When Picturing, observe the SOS Emanation instead of interpreting it. Interpreting can cause you to react by becoming upset, instead of recognizing the label and discovering what it is signaling.

Uneasiness or uncertainties expressed by understatements. These may occur when someone's fears make them uncomfortable. Instead of voicing their fears they understate what they feel. For example, imagine a fight where a loved one tells you they don't care about you, when in reality they love you dearly and fear losing you. They underrepresent their worry by presenting something that is really the polar opposite of what is going on—they understate their reality. This can lead you to react and assume that the other person does not care for you when in fact they are requesting that you notice their uncertainty and discomfort.

Exasperations are evaded through the use of emotion. This represents another kind of SOS Emanation, sent by others asking you to notice that something deeper is going. However, the other person does not state the unmet need that is causing them pain. Instead they deflect your attention with anger and evade sharing the true unmet need that is driving them. When Picturing, observe this signal so that you can draw out from the other person the unmet need driving it.

There are numerous other ways an SOS Emanation can be projected. However when the SOS Emanation is exhibited remember to picture (observe) the emanation neutrally because it is a clue, a hint, and a signal as to what the other person is requesting. Following are several exercises to help develop your skill with Picturing (observing) SOS Emanations, just follow the instructions!

SKILL BUILDER: 4

1) Receiving an SOS Emanation can be difficult. When faced with complaints, criticisms, or any other SOS Emanation, start by visualizing the other person as an SOS machine sending you Morse code. This helps you to focus on the signal, instead of your reaction to it. When an SOS Emanation surfaces remember that the other person is requesting something from you, they are sending you an observable clue.

There are other strategies that can help. Choose something you feel you can use to help you focus on the signal (the SOS Emanation), instead of your response and write it below:

_____
_____
_____
_____
_____
_____
_____

2) When noticing the SOS Emanation being sent, try your best not to respond by sending out your own SOS Emanation. To help with this, observe yourself and one other person for a week. Pay particular attention to high-stress moments. Make note of the Emanations you observe. (Remember, an Emanation can be any actions, behaviors or moods). Below is a list of Emanations that clue you into what is going on. You can add more Emanations to the list, as needed. Note what symbol you are using for yourself (either the ✗ or the ✓) and which one you are using for the other person:

✗ = _____   ✓ = _____

Emanations when experiencing high stress:

Blaming	Diverting	Exploding
Crying	Interrupting	Sulking
Preaching	Explaining	Using Sarcasm
_____	_____	_____
_____	_____	_____

3) As you look over your list of Emanations, choose a particularly high-stress one that you want to observe and practice removing, circle it and rate it below. My urge to react with this Emanation is usually:

Low   High
  1   2   3   4   5   6   7   8   9   10

4) In the sail of the boat, write your high-stress Emanation that you have committed to observing and removing for the next week.

Now visualize yourself sending the sailboat off to sea. The ocean takes *the sailboat and it floats away from you. As it travels the boat takes the Emanation out to sea and out of your life. As you visualize the boat sailing away, feel the release, hear yourself letting go; taste the difference, smell the sweet scent of liberation and see the new beginning. Every time you observe an occurrence of this high-stress Emanation you can visualize it sailing away in a boat. This provides you with one effective removal strategy. There are other strategies that can help. Think about what strategies will work for you, then choose one that you can use to remove the high stress emanation, list it below and then rate it:*

_____

_____

_____

_____

On a scale of 1-10, my rating of this removal strategy as practical and usable is:

Low									High
1	2	3	4	5	6	7	8	9	10

When selecting a removal strategy it is important to choose something that correlates to or exceeds your urge to react by displaying the Emanation. For example, if your urge to display the Emanation was high say a 9, and your rating for the removal strategy's practicality and usability was low say a 3, then your removal strategy may not produce the desired effects. You want to choose a removal strategy which rates higher than your urge to react by displaying the Emanation. This increases the effectiveness of your removal strategy.

BEHAVIOR

As you have read, when Picturing, the goal is to *observe* the Emanation, not to *interpret* it. By making a conscious effort to notice the Emanation, you empower yourself and your brain to remain fact-based. You want to notice, rather than interpret the Emanation, because *behavior is not universal*—diversity is always a factor in relationships. Acknowledging this means recognizing that not everyone will use the same actions to send the same message. Let's explore the feeling of frustration to illustrate and clarify the concept that behavior is not universal.

Often, when people feel frustrated, a variety of responses are possible. Some people smile, others cry. Some react by lashing out or hiding. The point is that we all express ourselves in different ways. This is why it is essential to remain focused on the facts, and not add your own preconceptions to a person's behavior. Remember, people may not only express themselves in different ways than you do but how they express themselves can also change over time.

PARTNERing is about staying open to these differences/changes and remembering that the meaning behind behavior is not universal. This is why Picturing is practiced by calmly observing—with neutrality—what you perceive in the moment. When you engage in PARTNER conversations, focus on the Emanation, not the message, because diversity exists and everyone will express themselves differently. Even when there are similarities in behavior, the drivers behind the behavior are individual and unique. PARTNERing facilitates your ability to uncover the other person's perspective. You can use the following skill builder to explore the unique ways behavior manifests itself in different individuals and to highlight the concept that behavior is not universal.

SKILL BUILDER: 5

To help uncover how unique and different we all are, answer the following questions:

1. *How do you like to unwind? What are your favorite ways to relax?*

   _____
   _____
   _____
   _____

2. *Pick someone close to you in your life. How does this person relax and unwind?*

   _____
   _____
   _____
   _____

3. *What are the similarities and differences:*

   _____
   _____
   _____
   _____

BODYTALK

When Picturing, what you see can trigger a reaction that may affect your ability to engage in fact-based observation. This is especially true when you observe SOS Emanations. One way to move past reacting, so that you can Picture with neutrality, is to notice your *BodyTalk*. This means applying your Picturing skills to yourself. *BodyTalk refers to the sensations you experience in your body.* For instance, noticing the physical sensation of having butterflies in your stomach may be one example of using BodyTalk to alert you to a high stress reaction. Because behavior is not universal you may find that some people feel butterflies when they are excited while others might not. It is vital to understand your own BodyTalk and comprehend the message it is sending you.

It is important to notice when your BodyTalk is signaling an increase in stress. When stress levels rises, analytic thinking, creative insight, and problem-solving abilities may all become impaired. Physically, stress stimulates heart rate, contracts blood vessels, and it may cause you to hold your breath. As blood vessels contract, the oxygen the brain receives is affected; this alters the brain's functioning. Think of oxygen as fuel for your brain, it keeps your brain processing smoothly. Without fuel your car ceases to function, the same is true of the brain. When oxygen flow to the brain is inhibited, the brain's ability to process is inhibited. This can negatively impact your ability to Picture (observe neutrally). One way to connect to a high-stress reaction is by being cognizant of your BodyTalk. When you are mindful of your BodyTalk you: become aware of when the brain's ability to process is affected by noticing the sensations in your body, and, you use your BodyTalk as a signal for reminding yourself to return to neutral observation (picturing).

Pay attention to your BodyTalk because it is a tool that can be used to enhance your ability to stay present to the other person's needs. For example, a missed deadline by an employee, or a conflict with your teen or significant other, can cause your stress level to rise and create anxiety. As your anxiety level elevates, you may begin to feel hot, and your heart may begin to race. By engaging in self-observation and noticing both of these symptoms, you are becoming more aware of your own BodyTalk. You can use this awareness to remind yourself to return to Picturing. With this in mind, let's work on identifying some BodyTalk indicators to enhance your ability to recognize them the next time they appear.

SKILL BUILDER: 6

Connecting to your BodyTalk helps you identify when you are reacting. When you react, it becomes difficult to observe the Emanation of others without interpreting a message. Noticing your BodyTalk is important since it is a signal you can use to remind yourself to step back, regroup, and return to observation.

1. What are your high-stress BodyTalk signals (if what you experience is not listed add it in next to the bullets)?

    - *Shaking*
    - *Turning red*
    - *Sweating*
    - *Nausea*
    - *Feeling hot*
    - *Butterflies*
    -
    -
    -
    -

2. One strategy to help with noticing BodyTalk is doing a heart-rate check. Let's practice this now. Place your hand over your heart and feel it beating, noticing if it's fast or normal. As you PARTNER you can do a heart-rate check to help you gauge your BodyTalk. If your heart rate is faster than normal, your body is telling you something.

3. Another strategy to become skilled at noticing BodyTalk is to practice noticing different BodyTalk indications. First, take a few moments to visualize something that causes you anxiety. As you visualize it, check your breathing and heart rate. Take a moment to shake this off. Now, take another moment and visualize someone you love. Picture them laughing hysterically. As you

imagine this, check your breathing and heart again. Note the difference in your BodyTalk during the two scenarios:

_____
_____
_____
_____

4. *There are other strategies that can help you notice your BodyTalk. Choose something that works for you and write your strategy below:*

_____
_____
_____
_____
_____
_____
_____
_____

RELEASE

RELEASE is focusing your attention to something more calming/soothing. When you feel your BodyTalk signaling high stress, it is important to *defuse* the reaction. This can be done by finding a way to release. To RELEASE you can use any of your five senses (sight, hearing, smell, taste, touch) or you can incorporate your mind/thoughts or body movement. The key is finding what works for you. More important than the technique is your use of it. When PARTNERing it is vital that you implement (use and practice) your selected RELEASE technique. Here are a few RELEASE techniques you can use to aid you in diffusing high-stress reactions in the moment:

Repeat the alphabet softly or count to 10 in your head.

Exercise your toes by wiggling them for 10 seconds.

Look around the room and describe it in your head as you swallow slowly.

Evoke the image of a place that calms you and visualize it for 10 seconds.

Allow yourself a moment to breathe deeply—in through the nose out through the mouth.

Squeeze the tips of your thumb and forefinger together and release.

Envision a word in your head that relaxes you such as "calm" or "peace."

To help understand the benefits of RELEASE, visualize yourself as a pressure cooker with the whistle going off. As you visualize your pressure rising, listen to, and feel, your BodyTalk. To let the pressure out, you need to turn the stove off. As you turn off your stove pay attention to your BodyTalk. Your RELEASE strategies work to help you turn your stove off thus releasing pressure. It's time to apply this to a simple exercise.

SKILL BUILDER: 7

On a scale of 1-10, my current ability to release high stress in the moment is:

Low   High
1   2   3   4   5   6   7   8   9   10

To move up half a point on the scale, I will recognize when my stress is increasing by tapping into the following BodyTalk indicators:

_____
_____
_____
_____
_____

I will manage a high stress reaction by applying the following release strategy (you can pick from the suggested RELEASE strategies, or you can choose some other strategy that works for you. The important thing is to have a strategy and practice it):

_____
_____
_____
_____
_____

On a scale of 1-10, my rating of this release strategy as calming/soothing is:

Low   High
1   2   3   4   5   6   7   8   9   10

When selecting a release strategy it is important to choose something that correlates to or exceeds your current ability to release high-stress. For example if your ability to release high stress was low and you rated your release strategy as low then your release strategy may not produce the desired effects. Choosing a release strategy rated higher than your ability to release high stress increases the effectiveness of your release strategy.

MINDTALK

In addition to noticing the physical changes occurring in your body, it is beneficial to observe the changes happening in your thoughts as well. This is your *MindTalk* and it refers to *the dialogue that goes on inside your head.* MindTalk can occur as you engage with another person in conversation. It can sometimes cause you to misinterpret the Emanations of others. The following section is designed to help you get the most out of your MindTalk.

MindTalk can be both *discouraging* and *encouraging*. When you interpret the Emanations of others as negative, this is usually due to discouraging MindTalk. Discouraging MindTalk induces stress, which affects your brain and in turn affects your ability to Picture. Encouraging MindTalk, on the other hand, can help to reduce stress, however it can also be destructive to your ability to Picture with neutrality. For example, if you have a missed deadline from an employee, encouraging MindTalk may tell you that the employee is capable of completing the task and not to worry—"This is probably a one-time incident," you say to yourself, and as such take no further action. By doing this you moved away from the observable behavior of the missed deadline, and applied your interpretation and perception. This could potentially be dangerous and destructive as the missed deadline might represent a request from that employee for help.

The key is to *assess* your MindTalk and the *impact* it can have. If the impact is found to be destructive then you apply the technique of *Reconstructing. Reconstructing is the process by which you renovate your thoughts by consciously recreating your MindTalk.* Reconstructing can be applied to both encouraging and discouraging MindTalk. You can Reconstruct your thoughts, thus opening you up to observe the signals/clues that other people are sending you more clearly. Remember, people are always communicating and sending off signals that give you a window into their perspective.

Take this scenario, for example. You are trying to help someone with a difficult task. The process becomes challenging and soon the other person begins to yell when speaking to you. Their sentences become short and they respond to you in a snappy manner. Your MindTalk may affect your Picturing, causing you to say to yourself: "They are disrespectful, rude, and don't appreciate my efforts." But this is not the only reaction you can have. You could Reconstruct your MindTalk by saying to yourself: "I can practice staying calm. The other person is sending me a signal through their behavior. Maybe they are requesting my support or it may be something else. Their actions are not directed at me personally."

Reconstructing is most effectively done by applying the GIFT principle:

Grow—Gauge the opportunity for self-improvement or learning in the situation.

Improve—Identify good intent.

Find—Focus on the possible request or the unmet need being communicated.

Transition—Take time to depersonalize.

MindTalk in need of Reconstructing represents an opportunity for growth—use the opportunity as a chance for improvement. To do this, validate your MindTalk, release the urge to judge it, and then Reconstruct it using the GIFT principle. You can validate your MindTalk by saying "Thank You" to it. By doing this you are acknowledging that your mind is sending you a message. Next, try not to judge your MindTalk—it is a natural part of your brain's attempt to process information, a clue into your own perspective. It represents your brain's unconscious effort to make sense of an observation and fit the observation into a schema/pattern. Instead, when you notice your MindTalk is reflecting interpretation, take a deep breath, and reconstruct it so you can return your attention to neutral observation.

Here is an example of how this is done. An employee comes to you and shares that a new project assignment is difficult to handle. As the employee shares this, you mentally tell yourself that the employee is capable of completing the project, despite having expressed their difficulties. You conclude that the employee may need to vent about the workload, but does not need any further support. Because you are learning to PARTNER you decide to investigate your MindTalk and assess its impact on the situation. This leads you to take a moment and PARTNER with this employee. As you do, you find out that their initial statement was really making a request for help, and was not just an opportunity to vent. In this case, it was beneficial for you to take a moment to reconstruct your MindTalk (to see the possible request) and to then move forward by providing support to the employee.

Lets look at another example to demonstrate the effect of your

MindTalk. Visualize the high-striker strongman games you often see played at carnivals. These games involve a participant hammering a small platform that, in turn, sends an eyebolt upward toward a bell. Imagine your MindTalk as the hammer and the bell as your goal. Is your MindTalk powerful and constructive enough to help you reach your goal? Does it keep you engaged in observing neutrally? Depending on your answer, you can choose to use the GIFT or RELEASE principles to bring you back to neutral observations. With a little practice using the GIFT principle
and reconstructing MindTalk, you can master the PARTNER method and start noticing a significant change in your relationships. Before moving on let's take a moment to practice.

SKILL BUILDER: 8

On a scale of 1-10, my current competency with reconstructing MindTalk is:

Competent									Incompetent
1	2	3	4	5	6	7	8	9	10

To help you grow in your ability to Reconstruct using MindTalk, practice using the GIFT principle. One way to remind yourself to do this is to wrap a small gift and leave it on your desk. Every time you notice it, recite the GIFT principle steps (Grow, Improve, Find, and Transition). Quickly think of a MindTalk message and practice Reconstructing it. There are other strategies that can help you remember to Reconstruct MindTalk and increase your skill. Choose something you feel you can use and write your strategy below:

_____
_____
_____
_____

Once you get comfortable noticing both BodyTalk and MindTalk, the next step is to recognize the important ways in which the two are linked. The state of your body, including your heart rate and stress level, can have a significant impact on your thoughts. In the same way, your thoughts, whether they are encouraging or discouraging, will feed-back into the state of your body. Because BodyTalk and MindTalk are so closely linked, it is important to stay attentive to both as you Picture (observe). Remember, you are a whole person, use your skills to be in tune with both your mind and body! Let's do some more practice exercises to finish up our work on Picturing. The remaining exercises will help build your Picturing skills and also get you ready for the next key, Articulation.

SKILL BUILDER: 9

1) You can sharpen your observation skills like you sharpen a pencil. For the next five days, take five minutes a day to Picture (observe) the actions of another person in your life. Look at that person's Emanations, both verbal and non-verbal. Write your observations in the space below.

Day 1: _____

_____

Day 2: _____

_____

Day 3: _____

_____

Day 4: _____

_____

Day 5: _____

_____

2) Another strategy you can use to sharpen your observation skills is—practice. When stopped at a red light, pretend like you are a news reporter. Look around and describe what you see as quickly as you can, focusing on the facts. This is something that you can turn into a game with your kids as well. There are other strategies you can use to sharpen your ability to observe. Choose something you feel you can use to help you become more observant and write your strategy below:

_____

_____

_____

_____

3) Notes, Thoughts, and Observations. In the space below, you can write what it is like to Picture. What were the challenges you faced when practicing observation? What worked? What will help you become more observant? What will help you to overcome interpretation? Finish by asking yourself: Why is Picturing beneficial?

_____
_____
_____
_____
_____
_____
_____
_____
_____
_____
_____
_____
_____
_____
_____

SKILL BUILDER: 10

Before moving onto the next key let's take a moment to practice the Picturing Skills you have learned.

1) Scenario: You are trying to help someone with a difficult task. The process is challenging, and soon the other person exclaims: "You are stupid and this process is ridiculous!"

Choose which of the statement represents Picturing without bias:

a. I am observing that that the other person is being childish and ridiculous!
b. I am observing that the other person is frustrated and cannot be worked with!
c. I am observing that the other person is difficult and rudely snapping at me!
d. I am observing that the other person is unable to understand things because they are stupid!
e. I am observing that the other person is communicating something right now, their words were: "This process is ridiculous".

2) Which statement represents an observation that is neutral?

a. The tree is my favorite color green.
b. The tress leaves are brownish and I like it better when they are green.
c. The tree is 5 feet.
d. The tree is 5 feet and has brownish leaves that I like.

3) Fill in the spaces below with reasons why Picturing is an important key in the process of strengthening your communication and relationships (the first one has been filled in for you as an example). Picturing is an important step in the process of improving communications and relationship because:

a. It provides information.
b.
c.
d.

Key Two: Articulate

As you progress through this book, you will begin to discover that each of the PARTNER keys build upon each other. In this chapter you will explore the "A." You will also discover how the "P" and "A" work together. Recall that the first key in the PARTNER model was *Picture*, and the goal was to learn how to observe neutrally. *Picture* lays the foundation for *Articulate*, which is the subject of this chapter. Here you will learn how to Articulate your Pictured observations.

In the PARTNER model, to Articulate is to *put your observations into words by describing the facts.* By definition, the facts include only what is *measurable* or *quantifiable*. Facts can be articulated in a variety of ways: verbally, when you are speaking directly with another person, or in written form, via e-mail or letters. As you Articulate, you put the events and/or actions you observed through Picturing into words, without including your own personal interpretation of things.

When Articulating what you observe, your goal is to be *objective* in describing the witnessed Emanation. A objective articulation sticks only to observable phenomena, and expresses the observed Emanation without the insertion of blame, interpretation, or assessment. In other words, when being objective your emotions or personal biases do not distort your words.

Your thoughts are a prequel to your words. This is why as you PARTNER you pay attention to your MindTalk (the dialogue that goes on inside your head). Whenever you catch your brain subconsciously adding interpretation or any form of bias, take a deep breath and reconstruct your thoughts by using the GIFT principle (Grow, Improve, Find, and Transition). Then, move forward and Articulate objectively.

Focusing on being objective is essential to your ability to Articulate. When you are *objective* you *relay your observations without BIAS.* In other words, you reflect only the Emanated signal, not the message you construe from the Emanation. By moving towards objectivity, your words become free of bias or judgment adjectives—you communicate objectively by not attaching what you feel or think to what you observe. It takes practice to be objective and Articulate only the emanated signal. BIAS can be hard to overcome, learning more about it is the first step towards improving your ability to Articulate objectively.

BIAS

To be objective it is important to understand how to speak or write in a BIAS free manner. In the previous chapter we touched briefly on how your personal interpretations can influence your ability to Picture. In this section, we take a deeper look at how BIAS can easily affect your PARTNER interactions.

One way that BIAS affects your interactions is when it seeps into dialogue, often unconsciously. The concept of BIAS as it relates to your Articulations can be summarized by exploring the following four principles:

Blaming the other person or bringing in the past
- Example: "It's your fault!"
- Example: "You never do anything right!"

Interpreting the other person's emotions
- Example: "You're angry right now!"

Assessing the other person's character
- Example: "You are a difficult person!"

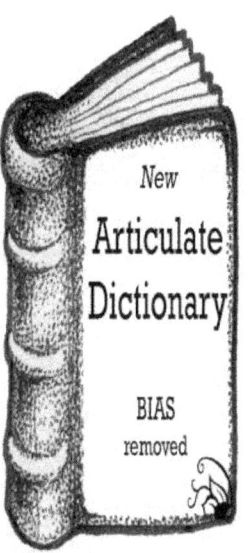

Selecting the other person's motives or thinking or option
- Example: "You are trying to hurt me!"
- Example: "You think I'm a fool!"
- Example: "Next time you should..."

When attempting to remain neutral, be selective with the adjectives and words that you choose. As part of removing your BIAS from your communication, you will specifically want to stay clear of using the words "never" and "always." Think of never/always as being "n/a" ("not applicable") to any interaction. Instead, focus on what has recently occurred without bringing in the past. Doing this enables you to stay in the moment, which helps you remain objective because you are not clouding the situation with past emotions or experiences. The following examples will help demonstrate, in a variety of contexts, how to Articulate what you Pictured without adding your BIAS:

1) Sample Statement: "My child was disrespectful last night. He did not come home before his 9 p.m. curfew. When he walked in at 9:10, he was irritated and uptight."
BIAS: "disrespectful" (assessing); "irritated and uptight" (interpreting)
Picturing: "My child's curfew is 9 p.m. (fact). My child came home 10 minutes after curfew last night" (fact).
Articulate: "I noticed you came home at 9:10 last night."

2) Sample Statement: "Jan is difficult; she missed the 5 p.m. deadline for the report. She did not come through for the team. She is lazy."
BIAS: "Difficult" (assessing); "did not come through for the team" (blaming); "lazy" (assessing)
Picturing: "The 5 p.m. deadline for Jan's report was missed (fact). I left the office at 6 p.m. and the report was still not in my inbox (measurable and quantifiable)."
Articulate: "When I left the office at six, your report was not in my inbox."

3) Sample Scenario: You and your teenager are in a disagreement. You tell your teen that the family car is not available tonight for use. Your teen kicks the wall.
BIAS: "You are angry and trying to upset me." (interpreting)
Picturing: My teen kicked the wall.
Reality: Your teen may be frustrated, angry and disappointed, or there could be another emotion at play; you don't know unless the other person names the emotion. You also don't know that your teen's intention was to upset you.

Articulate: "I saw you kick the wall."

4) Sample Scenario: Your co-worker comes to you and says, "I can't do this project."
BIAS: "My co-worker is frustrated." (interpreting)
Reality: Your co-worker may be stuck or overwhelmed, or there could be another emotion at play. You don't know unless the other person names the emotion, or tells you what is happening.
Picturing: "My co-worker said: I can't do this project."
Articulate: I heard you say, "You can't do this project."

These examples demonstrate that, when you Articulate, you focus on what has recently happened, you stay fact-based and objective by not including your BIAS when you speak.

As you Articulate, you want to remain conscious of the words you use. If you keep your sentences short, staying fact-based is more easily accomplished. Remember to tap into BodyTalk (sensations in your body) as it can cue you into when you are reacting and straying from being objective and/or neutral. As you practice Articulating in a BIAS free manner, you will hear the change in your day-to-day interactions with others—at home and at work. You will see doors of connection open and experience a transformation in your relationships. Now that you have an appetite for Articulating the facts, it's time to do some exercises to build your skills.

SKILL BUILDER: 1

Think of at least two recent statements you made, heard, or read in which BIAS was used and rewrite the statement using only the facts.

1) Recent Statement:

BIAS:

Fact Rewrite:

2) Recent Statement:

BIAS:

Fact Rewrite:

SKILL BUILDER: 2

1) On a scale of 1-10, I use BIAS:

Regularly   Never
1   2   3   4   5   6   7   8   9   10

2) To increase your effectiveness with removing BIAS for the next seven days, practice catching yourself in the act of using judgment adjectives or BIAS statements. Notice when this occurs and then make a mental check mark. Then, reconstruct in your mind and release, using an Empowering Motivational Statement (EMS) like the following: "I am one step closer to connecting to the truth." To create an EMS:

- *Begin with "I am" or "You are"*
- *Be specific*
- *Make it short*
- *Focus on strengths*

3) For an empowering motivational statement to work it needs to be repeated often. For example you can look yourself in the mirror, SMILE, and repeat your EMS. For this exercise, in the space below, write empowering motivational statements that you can commit to using.

- *"I am one step closer to connecting to the truth."*
-
-
-
-

UNLOCKING P = P

One way to Articulate objectively and avoid BIAS is to unlock P = P.

P = P refers to the tendency to make the person the problem ("Person = Problem"). When you use the formula "Person = Problem", the only way to address the problem is to change the person. With PARTNERing, the formula becomes P ≠ P. This effectively unlocks the person from the problem.

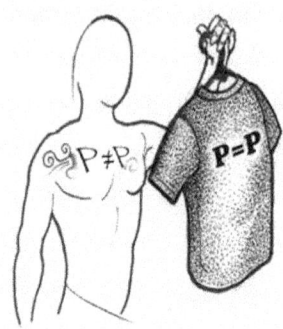

Think of P = P as the tattoo version of the person; it's very difficult and almost impossible to change. But, the P ≠ P version is more like a T-shirt. It can be removed and changed just like you would a shirt!

Consider the following examples, they demonstrate how to unlock the P= P relationship:

> *1) You look at your child's messy room and say to yourself, "My child is a slob."*
> *P = P (BIAS): Child = Slob.*
> *Unlocking P = P: "My child's room is messy." Child ≠ Slob*
> *(Tip: Focus on the problem, taking the problem outside the person and resisting the addition of an assessment to the person).*
>
> *2) Your colleague turns in a late report and you say: "he/she is lazy!"*
> *P = P (BIAS): Late report = Lazy co-worker*
> *Unlocking P = P: "The report was late." Late report ≠ Lazy co-worker*
> *(Tip: Focus on the problem using the facts, not by projecting a judgment label onto the person).*

The above examples highlight that, if you frame your child as a slob, then *they* must change. However, if you focus on the messy room, then the change is applied to the *situation* and not the *person*. In the same way, if you label your *co-worker* as lazy, then the only way for reports to be done on time is to get rid of the lazy employee. However, if you focus on the *incident* and not the person, you open the door to creative problem-solving.

When BIAS is used to associate the individual with a negative label, it will likely produce two things, 1) it will create defensiveness in the other person, and 2) it will frame the person as the problem instead of making allowances for changeable behavior. By combining the dilemma and the person into one, solving the problem requires changing the other person. This puts the other person on the defensive causing them to use high stress Emanations, SOS Emanations or BIAS to shield themselves. However, when you separate the challenge from the person, you make the problem something you and the other person can address together. It invites the other person to collaborate with you, and finding an option becomes more feasible as the focus shifts to what can be changed.

Take a moment to reflect on the benefits of Articulating this way. As you reflect, see the difference this shift in communication will make, hear how your conversations will change. Now, feel yourself becoming hungry for Articulating this way. It's time to fortify this shift with some skill building practice.

SKILL BUILDER: 3

Rewrite the following statements, unlocking the person from the problem.

1) Statement: "I have a mean neighbor; when she takes her pets for a walk, she handles them roughly and curses at them. She is an abusive pet owner."

Perceptions of the person:
_____

Rewrite, focusing on the problem instead of the person:
_____

2) Statement: "My child is very confrontational and resistant. He never does what is needed when asked. He always wants to know why and complains. He is forever looking for an easier way to do things. He makes things difficult for me and is extremely lazy."

Perceptions of the person:
_____
_____

Rewrite, focusing on the problem instead of the person:
_____
_____

3) Notes, Thoughts, Observations. In the space below write observations that helped you to unlock P = P. What was difficult? How will unlocking P = P be beneficial when you Articulate?

_____
_____
_____
_____

SKILL BUILDER: 4

1) During the next week, notice when you use P = P statements such as "You are frustrating. You make me angry. You need to change." In the space below, write one of your statements, then unlock the statement and reconstruct it to a P ≠ P statement.

P = P Statement:
_____
_____
_____
_____

P ≠ P Reconstruct:
_____
_____
_____
_____

2) On a scale of 1-10, my current competency with unraveling P = P is:

Competent   Incompetent
1   2   3   4   5   6   7   8   9   10

3) To help improve your ability with Unlocking P = P, consider creating a BIAS fund. Set up two jars: One gets money when you use a BIAS statement and the other collects your spare change. When you come home and empty your pockets reflect on your day, try to remember when you used a "You" statement that had BIAS (blame, interpretation, assessment, or selection). For each statement that you remember using, drop a coin in the appropriate container. The coins you put in the BIAS jar will have the greatest value, so start with the dollar coins and work your way down in value. If there is any change left when you are done, you can put that into the BIAS-free jar. At the end of the month, donate the BIAS jar (to a nearby school's supply fund, for example) and use the change in the BIAS-free jar to treat yourself (maybe to rent some movies you enjoy!). There are other strategies that can support this process. Choose something you feel you can use to help you reduce BIAS and write your strategy below:

_____
_____
_____
_____
_____
_____
_____
_____
_____
_____

THE DOMINO CYCLE

An important element in developing healthy PARTNER relationships is maintaining awareness of how other people's behaviors impact you, and also how your responses impact them. This pattern is called *The Domino Cycle*.

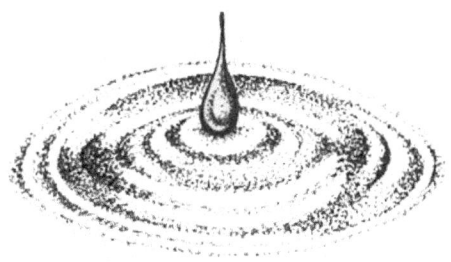

When Articulating your observations to other people, you draw them into a relationship with you. This means that when you Articulate, the words you choose, your tone of voice, and body posture all send a message to the other person. As you PARTNER you try to emanate in ways that invite collaboration. You don't want your Emanations to elicit defensiveness in others. To help with this it is important to be conscious of your Emanations (actions, behaviors, moods) as well as how the other person receives them (be cognizant of the Domino Cycle).

Let's look at an example. You noticed your teen came home 10 minutes after curfew. You Articulate these facts, but yell as you do so, crossing your arms sternly. The words are fact based but the message sent by the Emanations can cause your teen to become defensive. The teen may respond by rolling his eyes. This then escalates your frustration and you may yell as you become more upset. This impacts your teen by further inducing his stress and potentially leading him to walk away from you. This is an example of a *Destructive Domino Cycle*.

As you PARTNER you want to refrain from creating Destructive Domino Cycles and instead emphasize neutral observation and objective communication. You can do this by asking yourself: "Is my impact constructive or destructive in this situation?" If your answer is that the behavior is destructive then make adjustments, start by Reconstructing your MindTalk (dialogue in your head) and then follow this by adjusting your Emanations (actions, behaviors or moods). As you PARTNER pay attention to your Emanations—carefully choose your words, tone of voice and body posture. Remember your Emanations send messages! Let's look at the Domino Cycle and practice some PARTNERing skills so you can master them!

SKILL BUILDER: 5

1) For the next 21 days try to say thank you at least five times a day. When you say "Thank You," include a specific description of what the other person did. For example, instead of saying, "Thank you for dinner, it looks delicious," try being specific and say: "I see you made roast beef, carrots, and a special dressing for the salad, thank you." Make an effort to notice how the domino cycle plays out (is the impact constructive or destructive) and observe how the other person's reactions change as you highlight the specifics. At the end of 21 days, notice if there is a change in yourself and your relationships.

2) Another way to do this exercise is to pick a person you want to strengthen your relationship with. Make an effort to show that person appreciation at least five times a day. When you show appreciation, be detailed and include a behavior description. Observe how this impacts your relationship.

3) Notes, Thoughts, Observations. In the space below write: the benefits to being cognizant of the ripple effects of your actions (The Domino Cycle) and the impact your actions had.

_____
_____
_____
_____
_____
_____
_____
_____
_____
_____

SKILL BUILDER: 6

1) To enhance your ability to Picture and Articulate, use the space below to describe your current surroundings. Notice the colors and the way the space is laid out. What is the mood of the place? Is it comfortable? If you are in a room, do you find the lighting pleasant? What is your favorite feature, and what don't you like?

_____
_____
_____
_____
_____

2) Take a look at the description and draw a line through the adjectives that are not based on facts. In the space below, re-write the description using only the facts.

_____
_____
_____
_____
_____

3) Notes, Thoughts, and Observations: In the space below you can write observations such as: what helped you and what was difficult as you Articulated using only facts? How will focusing on being objective be beneficial when you articulate?

_____
_____
_____
_____
_____

SKILL BUILDER: 7

Before moving onto the next key let's take a moment to practice Picturing and Articulation. Remember when you Picture you observe neutrally and when you Articulate you objectively put these observations into words.

1) Scenario: You were at a baseball game today watching Tom play. After the game you and a friend were talking. Which of the following incorporates the PA in PARTNER?

    a.   Tom did not perform well at the game today.
    b.   Tom did not perform well at the game today because he dropped the ball 12 times.
    c.   Tom dropped the ball 12 times.

2) Scenario: You take your 4 year old niece out to lunch. At lunch she picked up her plate and it fell to the floor. After lunch you are describing to her mom what happened. Which of the following incorporates the PA in PARTNER?

    a.   Janet was a challenge today.
    b.   At lunch Janet aggressively threw her plate.
    c.   Today at lunch Janet picked up her plate when she was done eating, it fell on the floor and broke.

3) Take a moment to reflect on the importance of Picturing and Articulating in a PARTNER conversation. Fill in the spaces below with reasons why these are important keys (the first one has been filled in for you):

    a.   Bias free Articulation reduces defensiveness
    b.
    c.
    d.

Key Three: Realize

Having explored the "P" and the "A" of the PARTNER method, you are now ready to move on to the "R" in the interlocking PARTNER method. So far you have used *Picture* to unlock observations, and *Articulate* to unlock the use of words. The next stage in PARTNERing is *Realize*, a key used to unlock barriers in dialogue. Realize builds upon what you learned in Picture and Articulate. These steps are now followed with an inquiry about the Pictured observations. In other words, through the Realize key, you advance your conversations further as you draw out the other person's perspective with questions about your observations.

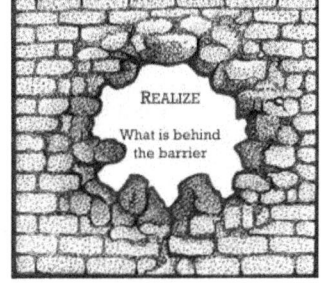

To *Realize* is to have the other person *identify the barrier(s) he or she faces.* Your goal is to figure out what is happening from the other person's viewpoint—to get more details by drawing out *their* perspective. This helps with identifying what the other person sees as the problem. This is accomplished by asking questions and listening to the other person's responses. As you listen, look for the clues that they give as this helps with obtaining their perspective. Also, invite the other person to share more of their story—this supports the other person by providing the opportunity for them to vent, share, unload, or explain their point of view. Let's explore some of the different ways to listen for the other person's perspective.

LISTENING

In the PARTNER method, you can listen from three levels: *Exclusively*, *Analytically*, or *Relationally*. These three modes of listening form the EAR spectrum, a tool that helps identify where your focus is as you listen. As you PARTNER you will use all three modes to listen holistically. As you practice becoming a more engaged listener, you will work on overcoming Exclusive and Analytical listening, while simultaneously incorporating Relational listening. Once you have obtained the skills from all three, you will activate the full EAR spectrum to increase your PARTNERing skills. Let's take a closer look at each level to help draw out how all three are manifested in PARTNER conversations.

Exclusive Listening. When in this mode of listening, your opinions and internal messages shape what you hear and receive from the other person. Hearing is hindered by your own perceptions and assessments. In other words, your hearing is blocked by BIAS. For example, as the other person communicates, the Exclusive listener may hear BIAS MindTalk (dialogue inside one's head) that contains blame (e.g., "It's all their fault"), interpretation (e.g., "The other person is angry"), assessment (e.g. "The other person is difficult") or that focuses on the selection of motives (e.g., "The other person must think I'm a fool to believe that").

A person who is caught in Exclusive listening is only able to notice the impact that the other person's Emanations (actions, behaviors or moods) are having on them; the focus is not on the other person's message. Exclusive listening is like listening to someone else with a set of headphones on, you only hear what's in your head, not the other person's Articulations or Emanations. If you are unable to move beyond Exclusive listening, you might get stuck focusing on the person as the problem (P = P). The Exclusive listener cannot hear what is being camouflaged, layered, underrepresented, unstated, and evaded.

Analytical Listening. The analytical listener focuses on the motions of listening; they follow the blueprint for listening but the analytical listener does not gather the underlying message from what is heard.

In this stage the headphones are off, and the Analytical listener tries to understand what the other person is communicating, but is not able to draw out the person's perspective. The needs and values being communicated by the other person remain a mystery—the Analytical listener is still unable to hear what is being camouflaged, layered, underrepresented, unstated, and evaded—even though the words of the other person are coming through. The Analytical Listener tries to connect to the other person's communication but this type of listener is not sure what to listen for, and is therefore unable to gather details from the other person's perspective. At this stage, the mechanics of listening are present but the messages are being missed. It's like knowing $E=mc^2$ (Einstein's theory of relativity), but not knowing how to apply the formula to physics.

Relational listening. The Relational listener is able to hear the other person's point of view, and focus on it. At this stage, understanding goes beyond words to comprehending the needs and values being communicated by the other person. With Relational listening you hear the other person's requests, clueing into their concerns, losses, uncertainties, uneasiness, and exasperations.

This is where Relational listening ends. The Relational listener can understand what is being communicated but, like the other two listeners, the Relational listener is limited. They are limited because without incorporating and overcoming the lessons and obstacles learned from Exclusive and Analytical listening they cannot use their understanding of the other person's drivers.

EAR Listening. The EAR listener simultaneously listens from all three levels, concurrently working on overcoming Exclusive and Analytical listening (an ongoing task), while incorporating Relational listening. With EAR listening you know how the other person's communication is affecting you (moving beyond Exclusive listening), you know how to use what you hear (moving beyond Analytical listening), and you can focus on the other person's perspective (moving beyond Relational listening). As an EAR listener you are conscious of the other person's communication, and you are competent in your ability to connect to the other person's perspective.

Engaging in EAR listening involves being empathetic and asking questions. *Being empathetic means that you emanate your sincere desire to connect.* This is done by creating a safe environment that encourages the other person to share. One way of doing this is asking the person: "What more is there, that you'd like to share?" This invites the other person to finish their thoughts and it sends the message that you really want to hear what they are sharing—you emanate *an aura of compassion, consideration, and sensitivity.*

As an EAR listener you are able to: discover the other person's viewpoint and address it. You listen with insight, which involves looking past what is being *presented* to see what is *being asked for.* Because you've mastered the mechanics of listening you are able to reflect the true message being communicated back to the other person for clarity. And you are able to combine this mastery with a deeper ability to look behind a person's shields.

When you successfully listen from the EAR you have moved beyond your own perspective; you are able to listen openly; you do not project your BIAS onto the other person. You move beyond your own story and you come closer toward connecting to the other person's story. The Chinese character for "Listen" embodies EAR listening. It is made up of the characters for eyes, ears, attention, and an open heart. Let's engage all these senses in the next skill building exercise!

SKILL BUILDER: 1

Directions: Read each scenario. Identify whether the statements/questions are reflective of "Exclusive" (focusing on self), "Analytical" (focus on words not meaning), "Relational" (focusing on the other person's point of view), or EAR listening (using the information) and why.

Scenario: You notice Meg is pacing back and forth. As you approach her, you hear her say, "If this bus doesn't come soon, I don't know what I will do!"

1. "Meg, when I hear you saying you don't know what you will do, that scares me."

Listening Type: _____
Why: _____
_____
_____

2. "Meg, I see you pacing but I am not sure what is happening right now."

Listening Type: _____
Why: _____
_____
_____

3. "Meg, I hear you saying you need the bus to come soon."

Listening Type: _____
Why: _____
_____

4. "Meg, your pacing is making it difficult for me to concentrate."

Listening Type: _____

Why: _____

_____

_____

5. "Meg, I heard you say you needed the bus to come soon. Is this because you are in a hurry or because it's cold out? Or perhaps you could share with me what else it might be?"

Listening Type: _____

Why: _____

_____

_____

6. "Meg, from the tone in your voice and by observing your actions, I wonder if you are nervous or impatient, or what else could it be?"

Listening Type: _____

Why: _____

_____

_____

SKILL BUILDER: 2

1) Where are you on the EAR (Exclusive, Analytical, and Relational) listening spectrum?

```
E ............................................A....................................................R
1     2     3     4     5     6     7     8     9     10
```

2) To move along the spectrum, set this intention: "I will be focused on the other person. I will listen in a BIAS free manner." Then turn on the news and, whenever you notice that you are listening from the "E" or the "A," repeat the intention until you are focused on the "R." Do this for one week. There are other strategies that can help increase your ability to listen. Choose something you feel you can use for the next week to move up the spectrum and write your strategy below:

_____

_____

_____

_____

_____

_____

3) Follow up a week later and ask yourself: "How have I moved up the EAR listening scale this week?" Note any observations in the space below.

_____

_____

_____

_____

_____

_____

THE POWER BEHIND QUESTIONS

We just explored how to listen to the speaker's response as you PARTNER. Responses are given when questions are asked, and questions are an important part of PARTNERing because the answers you get are clues from the other person. When you PARTNER you, show your desire to understand the other person through your choice of words, tone of voice, body posture, and your questions—how you frame your questions is important. You can ask questions in the traditional manner (e.g., "What is happening?"). Or, you can take the PARTNER approach in which you frame question as a request (e.g., "Tell me more about that..." or "Please explain..."). When framing your questions as requests, you are inviting the other person to open up and you are creating the opportunity for the other person to share their perspective.

In the PARTNER method, questions become your allies. They bring information and awareness to the surface. Take the following example to illustrate. If you and someone else were sitting in a room facing each other and were each asked to describe the room, your descriptions would not likely be the same. You would both have different accounts of the room based on your perspectives (yet you would both be describing the same room). To understand the other person's description, you would need to ask questions and seek further information. In the PARTNER method you create questions from a place of curiosity and wonder. Questions such as these are free of judgment, accusation, or condemnation (they are free of BIAS). Questions invite the other party to respond and share. Let's look at some of the different types of questions you can use to invite the other person to share.

EXPLORING IQ (INVITATION QUESTIONS)

Questions that invite sharing are called Invitation Questions ("IQs" for short). An IQ is a question that cannot be answered with a simple "Yes" or "No." IQs require a higher degree of detail—they extend an invitation to the other person to open up; to think and to share information with you. As the other person responds to your IQs use EAR listening to connect to their perspective. IQs and EAR listening help you bridge differences, they support your ability to understand the other person—together they help you see things from the other person's perspective, not just your own. Your IQs are like a bridge—they provide a way for the other person's perspective to travel over to you. When combined with EAR listening, IQs facilitate your ability to see the landscape on the other side as the other person shares.

An example of an IQ would be: "I'd like to take some time to check in with you, tell me how your day was..." (an open-ended question) verses: "Did you have a good day?" (a "Yes/No" question).

To be effective at PARTNERing, it is necessary to understand how to use IQs. An important element in any IQ is the *agenda*. The agenda outlines what you are asking about, the subject of the question. The agenda is followed with a request inviting the other person to share.

Without an agenda, responses can spiral off into other issues. The agenda sets a direction and tells the speaker what you are inquiring about and why. Having an agenda keeps things focused and moving forward.

Additionally, IQs involve exploring the "What," "When," or "How" of a situation. Remember, the goal of these questions is to draw out information. IQs encourage the person you're interacting with to provide more information. The following steps will assist you when asking IQs:

1. Open with the agenda.
2. End with a request for information.

The following statement demonstrates both of these steps: "I'd like to take some time to check in with you (agenda)… Tell me how your day was (request for information)…" As you use IQs, you will notice a difference in your communications because sharing will be increased. You will get more information. It's time for some practice with developing IQ's.

SKILL BUILDER: 3

1) In the space below, write two questions you use every day that are not Invitation Questions (IQs). Then rewrite the question as an IQ (see example below).

Non-IQ	IQ
Did your day go well?	How was your day? Tell me about your day? What was your day like today?

2) On a scale of 1-10, my current competency with using IQ vs. non-IQ is:

Competent   **Incompetent**
  1   2   3   4   5   6   7   8   9   10

3) Using Invitation Questions will benefit me in the following manner:

- *I will get more information*
-
-
-
-

4) You can further practice this method by creating an "IQ of the day." Every morning for the next week, choose an IQ that you want to use that day. Try to apply the IQ at least five times that day. For example, a common IQ question that you can practice at least five times tomorrow is: "What do you think of this weather?" This is one way that you can build your skill with IQs and move up one-half of a point on the scale (if you choose to do this skill builder, write your daily IQs below). There are other strategies that can help. Choose something you feel you can use to improve you skill with IQs and write your strategy below:

_____
_____
_____
_____
_____
_____
_____
_____
_____

TAKE 5

Now that you have spent some time exploring the power of Invitation Questions, let's add a few more strategies to help you develop a stronger connection through your inquiries.

When PARTNERing, it can be tempting to "Laundry List" questions by asking several at once. This is often an honest attempt to clarify what is being asked. However, it can make the situation more confusing and overwhelming. Resist the urge to ask numerous questions back to back. Instead, try posing only one at a time. For example, if you were to say: "I'd like to take some time to check in with you (agenda). Tell me how your day was (request for information)..." Laundry listing your questions would involve immediately following this inquiry with something like: "Tell me what you did, tell me if it was a good day, a bad day, or just an ordinary day, and tell me why, give me the details...". When you use IQs, you give the other person a chance to answer, if you Laundry List your questions it can overwhelm the other person. *It is perfectly acceptable to sit in silence while you wait for others to process the question and formulate their response.*

SKILL BUILDER: 4

1) What is your comfort level with silence? 5 seconds? 10 seconds? Notice where you are on the scale, in the next few days. When in conversation, (or after asking a question), how many seconds can you sit with silence before it feels uncomfortable (you will need to remember to count as you observe this)?

   1   2   3   4   5   6   7   8   9   10

2) When you feel uncomfortable, how do you emanate this? Do you Laundry-List your questions or do you engage in another Emanation (action, behavior)?

_____
_____
_____
_____
_____

3) Journal your thoughts as to what makes you feel comfortable or uncomfortable with silence in a conversation:

_____
_____
_____
_____
_____

4) One strategy to improve your comfort level is: taking deep breaths while waiting. As you do this pay attention to the other person's body language to notice if they are processing (focusing on the other person's body language and your breathing distracts you from the tension of waiting). This is just one strategy you can use to find comfort with silence, now choose a strategy that you can use and write it in the space below:

_____
_____
_____
_____
_____
_____
_____
_____
_____
_____
_____
_____

RealizeIQ

RealizeIQ's are open questions that invite the other person to share *their* perspective with you. The purpose of a RealizeIQ is to find out "Why" something is occurring—to draw out the *other person's viewpoint of the situation.* You do this by asking "What," "When," and "How" to encourage the person you're interacting with to provide information.

To use a RealizeIQ:

- *Picture:* Observe those around you to identify their emanations, which can be verbal (words, sounds) or non-verbal (actions). The *agenda* for a RealizeIQ is to gain more information about what was Pictured (observed).
- *Articulate:* Put your words into observations. Summarize the facts from Picturing.
- *Realize:* Develop questions from your observations that invite sharing and draw out the other person's perspective.

Let's look at some specific examples on how to use a RealizeIQ.

1) Parent Statement: "My child's curfew is 9 p.m. (fact). My child came home 10 minutes after curfew last night (observation)."
Question: "Did you come home after curfew last night?" (response is "Yes" or "No")
RealizeIQ: "I noticed you came home after curfew last night." (Articulating what was Pictured) "Tell me more about what happened?" (invites the other person to share information)

2) Co-worker Statement: "The 5 p.m. deadline was missed." (fact) "I left the office at 6 p.m. and Jan's report was still not in my inbox." (fact)
Question: "Jan, did you miss the report deadline?" (response is "Yes" or "No")

RealizeIQ: "When I left the office at 6 p.m. the report was not in my in box." (Articulating what is Pictured) Can you tell me what happened?" (invites an explanation)

When Realizing a*void framing your perceptions or assumptions as questions—i*n other words, refrain from adding your BIAS into your IQ. When BIAS enters a RealizeIQ, then your perception of the problem takes over the PARTNER interaction—you disguise your BIAS as a RealizeIQ instead of using the facts to draw out the other person's perspective. For example, if you see a co-worker or one of your kids pacing around and you ask a question that is:

Blaming the other person or bringing in the past
- Example: "Don't you see how your pacing could be irritating; tell me how your pacing is helping the situation?" (in this example you are blaming the other person indirectly)
- Example: "In the past when has pacing ever been helpful?"

Interpreting the other person's emotions
- Example: "Are you pacing because you are agitated?"

Assessing the other person's character
- Example: "Tell me are you pacing to upset me more, or make everyone irritated?"

Selecting the other person's motives or thinking
- Example: "Don't you think that by pacing you are ignoring how it's affecting everyone's ability to concentrate?"
- Example: "Do you think that I will let your pacing irritate me?"

In the previous examples what you are really doing is asking about your BIAS. You are asking about your own perspective, you are not asking the other person to share theirs. *BIAS leads the other person instead of empowering them to lead.* To avoid doing this, you might frame your RealizeIQ in the following way: "I see you are pacing back and forth, please tell me what is going on with you?" By focusing on the facts, you refrain from drawing conclusions about what the other person is experiencing, the motives behind their actions or what they feeling. Realizing is not about framing your perspective as a question. Realizing is about using IQ's to invite the other person to identify for you what is happening from their perspective. Remember, when you Realize you are creating opportunities for the other person to share.

When Realizing, keep an open mind while the other person responds to the RealizeIQ, (i.e., listen from your EAR). The answers you get may surprise you. As you PARTNER accept the other person's perspective. Reality, as you might see it, is not the goal. Remember the answers you get from the other person are clues into what they consider the issue, problem, or obstacle to be.

It's time to build your skill level! Ready, Set, Go!

SKILL BUILDER: 5

1) Reflect back on the last twenty four hours. In the space below describe a situation in which you could have used a RealizeIQ to empower another person to describe their perspective:

_____
_____
_____
_____
_____
_____

2) Use the space below to create a list of RealizeIQ's you could have used.

_____
_____
_____
_____
_____
_____

3) You can practice developing RealizeIQ's by using them in everyday situations. As you go about your day try to find as many opportunities as you can for creating and using RealizeIQ's. For example if you use your Picturing (observation) skills and notice that it's raining outside, you can create a RealizeIQ about this and use it for practice. You might engage a person in your office in conversation by asking, "I noticed it was raining outside (observation), how did this impact your commute today?" (invites sharing).

To improve your skill level, one strategy you can use is to commit to doing the following: use your RealizeIQ's in everyday situations for the next seven days. On the first day try to use at least one RealizeIQ, on the next day try to use two, and then the next day try to use three. This is one strategy you can use. Now choose a strategy that you can commit to and write it in the space below.

_____
_____
_____
_____
_____
_____
_____
_____
_____
_____
_____
_____
_____
_____
_____
_____
_____

BOND

When your RealizeIQ is not greeted with the sharing of information, this is a clue that the other person needs support, encouragement, or reinforcement before they will share. If this happens you may wish to create a BOND to help improve the situation. When you create a BOND, you invite sharing by expressing to the other person your sincere desire to connect and understand—you offer the other person a reason to open up. There are four parts to building a BOND:

Base—Create a base by stating the facts that you've Pictured. For example:
- "You came home late."

Offer—Share your feelings, BodyTalk or Emanation. For example:
- "While waiting, I felt worried and nervous."
- "When I saw you, my heart skipped a beat."
- "When you walked in, I let out a sigh of relief."

Nurture—others by building a bridge for why you want to share. For example:
- "...because understanding you is important."

Delve—with your question. For example:
- "Tell me what happened to cause you to be late."

When you build a BOND you motivate the other person to share. Subsequently, you share what happened and how it impacted you. Finally, you let people know they are important and you care about them. This is used as a springboard to spur the other person's willingness to share more information with you.

Here's another scenario. You have spent all summer taking care of your yard and making it beautiful. One day, after the kids next door get done playing basketball, you notice that their ball has crushed your flowers and the kids have trampled your plants. Your garden is destroyed. You want to open the doors of communication and understand the kids' perspectives. First, you may need to take a moment to breathe and RELEASE (a time out to give the brain the oxygen it needs for processing), then, you can create a bond by initiating the following dialogue:

B—"When the flowers were crushed..."
O—"...I felt disappointed."
N—"Since I want everyone to understand what happened..."
D—"...please share your perspective with me."

Creating a BOND is especially helpful if the other person responds to your RealizeIQ with something other than the sharing of information. When this occurs the other person does not respond to your RealizeIQ by giving you the details. Instead they respond to your Realize IQ by Emanating in the following manner, giving you a CLUE that a BOND is needed:

Camouflage their concerns with criticisms or complaints
- Example: "You only want to know what occurred so that you can blame me."
- Example: "You don't really want to know the truth, all you ever do is interpret what I say and turn it into something else."

Layer their loss beneath labels
- Example: "You are rude, I'm not answering your questions, you're not asking because you really want to understand me, you don't care about how I feel."
- Example: "You are an awful person, you always question me."

Underestimate or underrepresent their uneasiness or uncertainties
- Example: "I don't want to talk about it."
- Example: "It's no big deal, nothing is wrong."

Evade sharing their exasperation by using emotion and projecting onto you

- Example: "I'm so angry that you would ask me questions, you are only doing this so you could tell me what to do."

When using BONDs, you nurture and build bridges of connection. To do this you speak with sincerity and vulnerability by telling other people why they matter to you, and, why you want them to answer your question (you speak from the heart). The reasons you give will build connection by revealing to the other person how important they are to you. A BOND is an expression of your care and concern, and it requires that you move past your initial reactions and focus on using words that invite relationship and sharing. When you build connection and create a BOND, choose the words that describe your emotions wisely. Select words that reflect your feelings—refrain from selecting words that point fingers at the other party indirectly.

For example, there is a difference between saying "I feel alone" and "I feel abandoned." The latter implies that the other person left you (blame), while expressing "aloneness" shows your ownership of your feelings. Similarly, stating "I feel frustrated," versus "I feel provoked" demonstrates the same concept. "Provoked" implies that the other person is purposely upsetting you, while "frustrated" only implies what you experienced about what occurred. When sharing your feelings, stay away from indirect finger pointing with your words, instead choose words that reflect your emotions, not your biases.

Let's pause here for a moment to reinforce the PARTNER skills you developed during this chapter with a few quick skill builders.

SKILL BUILDER: 6

Direction: Look at the following scenario and rewrite the statement using the BOND concept. Incorporate the key components: Base (facts), Offer (feeling), Nurture (bridge) and Delve (question).

1) You are part of a team. There is a big project due and it's taking a long time to complete. While conversing with another co-worker, he complains: "I hate this project. Nobody helps me and I can't do it. It's taking too much time and it's way too difficult." Engage your co-worker in a PARTNER relationship by building a BOND:

B — _____

O — _____

N — _____

D — _____

2) You and a friend are having a PARTNER discussion. You ask a RealizeIQ (question to draw out the other person's perspective), but instead of responding by sharing information your friend yells "You're always questioning me!" Which of the following (a or b) incorporates a BOND statement (as you read, identify the base, offer, nurture and delve)?

    a. When you yell at me (___) I feel frustrated (___) because I assume you don't care (___), next time will you communicate your frustrations without yelling (___)?

b. When I am yelled at (____), I feel frustrated (____) because we are friends (____), let's talk about how we can communicate our frustrations (____)?

3) Create a BOND statement about the following. You and someone close to you get into a fight over your life choices. During a verbal exchange the other person yells "You are so stupid, I cannot deal with this anymore!"

Base (fact): When _____

Offer (feeling): I feel _____

Nurture (reason/motivator): because_____

Delve (request): _____

SKILL BUILDER: 7

1) List BIAS words that might be mistaken for a feeling. Next to the word, note feeling word(s) that you can use instead.

BIAS Word	Replacement Emotion
provoked	frustrated, puzzled, overwhelmed
understood	empowered, appreciative, satisfied

2) Select a word for the list to work on for the next week then fill in the following:

For the next week, I will work on replacing this BIAS word:
_____
_____

I will replace it with:
_____
_____

3) Read each statement. Check the "Yes" or "No" box.

Question	Yes	No
1. I wait for others to finish what they are saying without interruptions before I speak.		
2. I ignore outside distractions and focus on the speaker when I am listening.		
3. After a conversation, I remember what was said to me.		
4. When in doubt, I ask questions to increase my understanding.		
5. I pay attention to other people's body language when they are talking to me.		
6. I notice other people's tone of voice when they speak to me.		
7. I refrain from multi-tasking when listening. I give the speaker my full attention.		
8. If there is a pause, I refrain from finishing the sentences of the speaker.		
9. Even if I disagree with the speaker, I avoid tuning him or her out.		
10. When listening, I try to understand the message behind behavior.		

The "Yes" answers show the listening skills you already have. The "No" responses highlight areas for improvement.

4) Looking at your "Yes" and "No" answers, create a list of at least 10 ways you can improve your listening.

I commit to improving my listening skills by:

    1.   No longer multi-tasking when listening.
    2.

3. _____
4. _____
5. _____
6. _____
7. _____
8. _____
9. _____
10. _____

SKILL BUILDER: 8

Before moving onto the next key let's take a moment to practice Picturing, Articulation, and Realizing. Remember when you Picture you observe neutrally; when you Articulate you put your observations into words, and, when you Realize, you unlock the barrier as the other person sees it. Use the following skill building exercise to help you incorporate and review the first three elements of the PARTNER method.

1) You walk into the office and hear a co-worker saying "This project is complicated." Which of the following incorporates the PAR?

    a.   "I hear you saying that the project is complicated, come into my office and tell me more."
    b.   "I know it's a complicated project but you can do it."
    c.   "If you have problems with a project you need to come to me not talk with others about it."

2) You are teaching your son to do laundry. He comes to you and says "I don't want to do my laundry!" Which of the following incorporates the PAR?

    a.   "Don't you think it's important to have clean clothes?"
    b.   "If you don't do your laundry, what will you wear?"
    c.   "I hear you saying that you're not wanting to do your laundry, please share with me the reason behind this statement?"

3) Take a moment to reflect on the importance of Picturing, Articulating, and Realizing in a PARTNER conversation. Next, fill in the spaces below with reasons why these are important keys in the process of strengthening your communication and relationships (the first one has been filled in for you as an example). Realizing is an important step in the process of improving communications and relationship because:

    a. IQ's that are fact based reduce defensiveness and open the door for the other person's perspective to surface.
    b.
    c.
    d.

Key Four: Test

So far you have explored the "PAR" in the PARTNER method. In this chapter you will read about how the "T" fits into the model, and you will learn how the "PAR" and the "T" work together. You have already learned to use *Picture* to unlock observations, *Articulate* to unlock the use of words, and *Realize* to unlock the other person's perspective. The next key of the PARTNER model is *Test*. With the Test key you will learn to use the details gathered from your IQs to ask about and unlock the *Unmet* needs of another person. In PARTNER conversations, *Unmets are the unaddressed concerns or violated values that motivate each person.* Simply stated, Unmets motivate and drive behavior. They are the unconscious reason behind why a behavior surfaces—the reason a person wants something. Even though we all have Unmets they are difficult to identify. The Unmet can be difficult to uncover since it is often shielded—camouflaged, layered beneath or covered by another action or behavior.

Finding the Unmet is like doing a puzzle. When solving a puzzle you try to figure out the relationships between the pieces so you can see how they all fit together. You investigate where the pieces go, by testing them out to find where they fit. This is done by looking for clues amongst the shapes, and then trying out the pieces to see if you've discovered the appropriate fit. If it turns out the piece does not fit then you continue to explore. Engaging in Testing (looking for the Unmet) is a bit like doing a puzzle without a box, or doing one that is scrambled like a slide puzzle. You may have pieces in front of you (giving you a general sense of what is going on) but you don't know ahead of time what the final image (the Unmet) is, and you won't know how it's all going to be brought together unless you Test.

Remember, in the Test stage of a conversation you are doing something very similar to putting a puzzle together. You are using specific questions to fit together pieces of information so that you can discover the Unmet. Doing a puzzle takes patience, and, in the same way that a puzzle takes time to put together, so does finding the Unmet—be gentle and patient when you engage in Testing. Before exploring how to engage in Testing with another person, let's take a moment to understand what the different types of Unmets are like. Unmets can be categorized in the following ways:

- *Mental*— Exhibiting the desire for self-worth, self-respect, and a sense of achievement— wanting to become the person you feel that you are capable of becoming, feeling as though you have achieved what you consider to be your very best.
- *Physical*— Indicating a desire for the basic needs for survival (e.g., food, water, or sleep). At times people's physical Unmets can drive their behavior. Have you ever noticed that people can get short-tempered when they are hungry? Or perhaps that they get forgetful when they have not had enough sleep?
- *Spiritual*— Showing a desire for meaning in life through relationships with God and others. The need for love, belonging, and connection with family and friends are examples of Unmet spiritual needs.

It's time to do a quick practice!

Unlocking the Power of Words

SKILL BUILDER: 1

1) Look at the list of Unmets below and circle the ones that currently need addressing in your life.

Possible Unmets include:

- *Acceptance*
- *Independence*
- *Creativity*
- *Fairness*
- *Rest*
- *Organization*
- *Stability*
- *Consideration*

- *Security*
- *Choice*
- *Celebration*
- *Challenge*
- *Friendship*
- *Contribution*
- *Opportunity*
- *Respect*

2) In the space below, include other Unmets that may drive a person's actions. What Unmets could you look for in yourself and others?

_____
_____
_____
_____
_____
_____
_____
_____
_____
_____

TestIQs

To put a puzzle together you look for clues to find where the pieces fit—you investigate. In order to find the Unmet need, summarize the facts and the information you observed from the Picture stage and combine them with the information gathered from the Realize stage. You draw from the "P" and the "R" and use your skill from the "A" to create an IQ aimed at uncovering the Unmet. In the Test stage of a conversation your questions are focused on identifying the Unmet need(s) driving the other person's action(s). Remember that, like a puzzle, the image (Unmet) won't be clear until you Test (put the puzzle pieces together using your questions). The IQs that you use in this stage of PARTNERing are called TestIQs

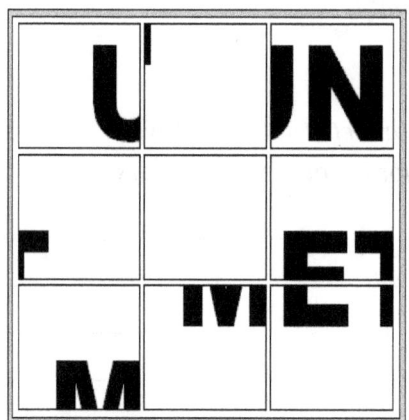

Return now to the image of the slide puzzle (left), the pieces of the illustration are there, but they are not yet where they need to be, so the image (the Unmet) is shielded from your view. To identify the image (find the unmet) the pieces need to be moved around. This takes time and is often difficult. Luckily, there are tools you can use. TestIQs are an instrument for sliding the puzzle pieces around. As you employ TestIQs the other person begins to clarify their camouflaged concerns, label their layered losses, unveil their unstated uncertainties, and explain their exasperations. With the help of TestIQs they begin to clue into their Unmet and share it with you.

To unlock the unmet it is helpful to state a clear agenda in the TestIQ. You can create an agenda to show your desire to connect and comprehend in two ways. First, you can show a desire to connect by using phrases such as "To help me connect to what's happening..." Opening TestIQs with phrases similar to this demonstrates that you want to connect the other person. It tells the other person that their whole person— their perceptions and their perspectives— really matter to you. Second, you can show a desire to comprehend the other person (their actions and drivers) by summarizing what you observed during Picturing.

In addition to having an agenda you want to do the following with TestIQs: offer the other person, two possible Unmet options and end the IQ with a request for the person to think deeper. Let's explore this with an example. Imagine that you suggest an activity to your child or co-worker, to which they respond bluntly: "This is stupid!" Instead of reacting impulsively to this situation with BIAS use your PARTNER skills, Reconstruct your thinking, and pause to ask yourself: "What is the Unmet that is driving this person?" Perhaps it is a request for help or the desire to feel independent. Perhaps it is something else altogether, the goal is to Test and find out (remember you may have bits of information, but you don't have access to the entire puzzle image). To help uncover the Unmet, apply TestIQs by using the following formula:

TestIQ = Agenda + Offer1 + Offer 2 + Invitation Question

The above formula is illustrated in the following examples:

1) "To help me connect to what's happening (Agenda), is it that you would like help (Offer 1), or is it that you would like feedback (Offer 2) or, what else could it be (invitation question— extending a request to the other person to think deeper)?"

2) "I heard you say that this is stupid, I'd like to understand this (Agenda), is it that you would like help (Offer 1), or is it that you would like feedback (Offer 2) or, what else could it be (invitation question— extending a request to the other person to think deeper)?"

As you PARTNER and use TestIQs remember to use EAR listening so that you can hear the clues that the other person sends about their Unmet. Remember to exercise empathy here, try to feel where the other person is coming from and infuse your interactions with patience—finding the Unmet can take time! To help reinforce your skill with TestIQs let's take a moment for a skill builder.

SKILL BUILDER: 2

Look at the list below and choose what is missing from the following TestIQs and rewrite them using the TestIQ formula (TestIQ = Agenda + Offer1 + Offer 2 + Invitation Question):

1) "Is there a need for acceptance, or is that you want help or what else could it be?"

_____

_____

_____

_____

2) "Let me see if I understand, you are frustrated or maybe you are in need to relax?"

_____

_____

_____

_____

3) "You are hungry and tired, am I correct?"

_____

_____

_____

_____

SHIELD

Earlier you learned that the Unmet can be difficult to uncover because it can be camouflaged, layered beneath, or covered by another action or behavior. In other words the Unmet is often *Shielded* from view. *Shields are what the other person uses to deflect your attention away from the Unmet.* Shields cover the Unmet and draw your attention in a different direction—this is why finding the Unmet can be puzzling. Shields can take many forms: they can take the form of a statement, behavior, action or option. No matter what form they take Shields clue you into the unmet.

If this description of a Shield sounds familiar, that is because the Shield is related to the notion of *Emanation* discussed in Key One. Recall that *Emanations are actions, behaviors, or moods* and function in two primary ways: first, as a clue to signal, alert, and draw attention, and second, to communicate a specific message. Further, they may appear as *SOS Emanations* through complaints, criticisms, labels, or finger pointing. When a Shield is emanated it protects or distorts the Unmet so that you are faced with a puzzle. A puzzle's image is distorted when the pieces are separated or scrambled and will remain distorted until you test out the pieces to find where they fit. The same is true of the Unmet. The tendency to shield the unmet is unconscious. When you PARTNER and the other person unconsciously protects their Unmet, it is said that they are using a Shield or shielding the Unmet.

When you Picture (observe) your focus is not on reacting to the SOS Emanation but on noticing the request that the SOS Emanation signals. The same principle applies here, when you Test the focus is not on the Shield, it is on discovering the Unmet covered by the Shield. Let's explore this with an example. Envision that you and your teenager are in a disagreement. You tell your teen that the family car is not available for use tonight. Your teen kicks the wall (Emanation) and yells: "You are so irritating! I can't stand you or this family!" (Shield) In this case, the Unmet might be the teen wanting friendship, autonomy, control, freedom, or to have fun. However, this is not necessarily what the teen expressed in the argument. The teen presented you with a puzzle—an emanated shield. This shield is a clue that something deeper is going on, however it is not clear, what the deeper issue is. Instead of trying to interpret or assess (from your perspective) what the Unmet is, you ask the teen to uncover it for you. You engage in PARTNERing and use TestIQs to find the unmet that is being shielded.

Let's explore this scenario further by Testing using the TestIQ formula (*TestIQ = Agenda + Offer1 + Offer 2 + Invitation Question*). As you PARTNER with your teen, respond by Testing for the Unmet in your teen by stating: "I saw you kick the wall and heard you say that you can't stand me or this family, is this because you wanted to hang with your friends (Offer1) or because you need a break (Offer2) or what else might it be?" Another way to ask this question is: "Do you find this to be irritating because you wanted to hang with your friends (Offer1), or because you need a break (Offer2) or, what else might it be?" (This question incorporates the information given by the teen)

The above dialogue focuses on the Unmet, instead of the Shield—it seeks the teen's perspective. In addition, by offering possibilities (giving the teen choice) and ending with a request (offering choice again), the TestIQ supported the teen in leading the way, thus it opened the conversation to follow the path created by the teen. Offering possibilities and ending with an invitation to think deeper keeps you from projecting your own perspective, interpretation, or assessment. TestIQs keep BIAS out of your PARTNERing and opens the door for the other person, in this case the teen, to clarify, label, unveil, or explain their Unmet.

Let's look at another example, this time exploring a conversation between two neighbors. In this example Neighbor 2 uses the PARTNER model:

Neighbor1: "Tom's dog is a nuisance!"
Neighbor2: "I heard you say that Tom's dog is a nuisance (Picture

and Articulate), tell me what has been going on (RealizeIQ)?"

Neighbor1: "The dog barks all the time, it should be someplace where it won't disturb anyone. I want Tom's dog taken to the pound (Shield)."

Neighbor2: "The dog's barking affects you because it disturbs your quiet (offer 1), or because it interrupts family time (offer 2), or what else could it be?

Neighbor1: "I want Tom's dog taken to the pound (Shield). Then it would be quiet and I could sleep." (clue/driver as to the Unmet)

By addressing the Unmet desire for peace and quiet, the Shield that was presented was not emphasized. Rather, the focus became the underlying Unmet. Focusing on the Shield (in this case, the option of taking the dog to the pound), narrows the avenues for dealing with the unmet (in this case there would be only one avenue for dealing with the problem: getting rid of the dog). However, by focusing on the Unmet behind the Shield (peace and quiet), the range of options is expanded. By looking at the Unmet, the options for addressing the barrier increase—the horizon of possibility expands.

Addressing the Unmet increases creativity and collaboration. In the above example, focusing on peace and quiet generates discussion. The discussion can cover what time frames the dog's barking effects sleep, the possible use of earplugs, keeping the dog inside during sleeping hours, etc. Multiple options for addressing the barrier are revealed when the focus is shifted from the Shield to what is Unmet. To help reinforce these skills let's do a quick skill builder focused on practicing TestIQs.

SKILL BUILDER: 3

Take a look at the following scenario and create a TestIQ that focuses on the Unmet hidden by the Shield. Remember, TestIQs incorporate the following formula: TestIQ = Agenda + Offer1 + Offer2 + Invitation Question.

A friend calls you crying. You open your conversation with a RealizeIQ that incorporates both Picturing and Articulation. You say: "I hear you are crying, tell me what is driving this?" Your friend responds with the following: "It's my birthday, and as usual you did not call. I always remember your birthday and I'm always there for you. I just don't understand why you are so inconsiderate. Maybe we just should not be friends!"

In an attempt to find the unmet you say:

EMOTIONS IN OTHERS

As you PARTNER you may encounter strong emotions. It is important to remember that *emotions are not the cause they are the symptom.* The Unmet is the cause and this where you focus in a PARTNER dialogue—the cause not the symptom. When strong emotions surface, ask the other person to name their emotions for you so that you can follow up and find out the underlying driver for that emotion.

Before you are able to get to the Unmet driving the emotion, it is important to test the waters and discover what the emotion is. Stay clear of naming the other person's emotions for them, encourage them to identify their own emotion/s—this helps limit projections of your own interpretation or assessment onto the PARTNER interaction, it limits BIAS. As part of not projecting your interpretation onto the other person you encourage them to name their own feelings using a TestIQ.

The TestIQ offers the other person multiple feeling options, thus encouraging them to identify their own emotion—try, to offer two emotions that are not the same. For example if you were to say "I want to understand what you are feeling (agenda) is it that you are annoyed (emotion offer1) or is it that you are irritated (emotion offer2), or what else are possible emotions you are experiencing (invitation to think deeper)?" You are asking about the same emotion in varying degrees. This can lead the other person, instead of letting them lead you. Instead you can ask, "I want to understand what you are feeling (agenda) is it that you are annoyed (emotion offer1) or is it that you are hurt (emotion offer2), or what else are possible emotions you are experiencing (invitation to think deeper)?" Remember you want to PARTNER with and empower the other person to lead.

As part of empowering the other person you accept the label they give to their emotions. As you PARTNER, it is the other person who names their emotions, not you. This means as you PARTNER you refrain from making statements like "What you are feeling is...." or "That's not what you are feeling, you are really feeling....." Open the door for the other person to clarify for themselves what they are feeling; support their ability to label/name their emotion. After they label their emotion, incorporate this new information into the TestIQ and ask about the unmet behind the emotion.

There are many reasons why emotions surface. The emotion may have surfaced due to a concern, loss, uncertainty or exasperation. By using TestIQs, and inviting the other person to name their emotion, you are empowering the other person. Once they label their emotion(s) you use TestIQs to seek out the unmet that lead to the emotion (or caused the emotion to surface). By using TestIQs you invite the other person to reveal their emotions, explain them, and uncover the drivers behind them. The other person leads the way in a PARTNER conversation, they learn to understand themselves and they learn to share this with you. Let's practice testing for emotions.

SKILL BUILDER: 4

Look at the following scenario and create a TestIQ that focuses on discovering the other person's emotional state. Remember, TestIQs incorporate the following formula: TestIQ = Agenda + Offer1 + Offer2 + Invitation Question.

Scenario: Your daughter just came home from school. You notice that she is stomping and throwing things. She tells you that she despises her math teacher. You want to understand her feelings so you ask:

SKILL BUILDER: 5

During the next twenty four hours ask at least five people what they are feeling. You can create a TestIQ geared toward uncovering a person's emotion on any topic. For example you can create a TestIQ to uncover the other person's emotion about the weather (agenda). You can ask a co-worker: "I noticed it's sunny outside, does this leave you feeling hopeful, or does it make you happy, or what else does it make you feel?" Use the space below to journal about your experience or to create a list of possible TestIQs (questions to uncover emotions or the unmet) to use.

DISCOVERY

In previous chapters, you explored an important fact—behavior is not universal. This applies to the Unmet as well. As you Test, avoid making any assumptions (interpreting or selecting what the other person wants, needs, or expects). Instead, gather information from the other person. Allow them to clarify, label, unveil, and express what they want, need or expect. How people define their Unmet will vary from one individual to the next.

Part of Testing is not only uncovering the Unmet but identifying what it means. Once the unmet is identified, it is then necessary to *discover* what this means to the other person. When engaging in Testing, use your questions to gather from the other person a description of what meeting their Unmet looks like to them. You are looking for the other person to clue you into their perspective. Doing this supports the next 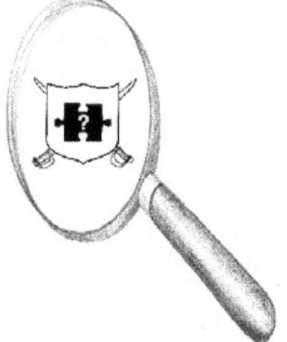 key in the model where options for meeting the Unmet are generated.

To help illuminate this concept let's look at the Unmet of "belonging." Some people may define belonging as having dinner with friends once a week, others may define belonging as getting a present on their birthday, yet another may define belonging as a weekly phone call. Remember, due to diversity, behaviors and definitions are not universal. This is why it's important to ask questions during the Test phase. By asking, you invite the other person to define for themselves the actions and behaviors that will address their Unmet.

When you ask and receive an answer, it is also important to accept the person's description as *their* truth. For example, to some, love is getting flowers once a week, having the car washed, getting a card, or hearing the words "I love you." This may not be how you define being shown love but you accept the other person's definition as their truth. Even if you don't understand the other person's perspective, when they clue you into it accept it, use EAR listening to hear what is being revealed to you. Now it's your turn to put this PARTNER skill to use! Let's practice overcoming Shielding with an exercise.

SKILL BUILDER: 6

1) Earlier (on page 93) you circled unmets that need addressing in your life. In the space below write out the Shields you use to cover your unmet.

_____
_____
_____
_____
_____

2) During the next week, try to identify when you are using a Shield to cover an Unmet. Place a checkmark in the space below for every instance, and then add them up.

_____
_____
_____

3) Circle where you fall on the scale below. I shield my Unmet:

Most of the time Never
 1 2 3 4 5 6 7 8 9 10

4) The disadvantage of communicating my Shield is:

_____
_____
_____
_____
_____

5) The advantage of communicating my Unmet and not shielding it is:

_____

_____

_____

_____

_____

_____

6) To communicate my Unmet instead of my Shield I will:

_____

_____

_____

_____

_____

_____

7) Take a moment to reflect on how far you've come with the PARTNER model. As you reflect, focus on how using the PARTNER approach can create more harmony in all your relationships. Try to feel the bonds of communication becoming stronger, see the connections becoming more fluid, and hear the contentment in the other person's voice. As you practice PARTNERing it will become easier for you to digest this new way of interacting.

_____

_____

_____

_____

_____

_____

SKILL BUILDER: 7

Before moving onto the next key let's take a moment to practice Picturing, Articulation, Realizing and Testing. Remember, when you Picture you observe neutrally, and when you Articulate you put your observations into words. When you Realize you unlock the barrier as the other person sees it, and when you Test you uncover the Unmet. Put these PARTNER keys to use with the following scenario.

Scenario: You and a co-worker are working on a big project. The deadline is looming and there is still a great deal to do. In addition to the stress of this project your co-worker has also shared that he is having family trouble. Today while at your desk you hear a loud noise. As you turn around you see your co-worker slamming their phone down. In addition you hear your co-worker exclaiming: "This is all too much for me right now!"

1) What are the facts (remember to stick to only what you observed today)?

_____
_____
_____
_____
_____

2) What is a RealizeIQ that you could use to invite your co-worker to share their perspective?

_____
_____
_____
_____
_____

3) What is a TestIQ to draw out their emotion?

_____
_____
_____
_____
_____

4) Reflect on the scenario and create a list of at least five unmets that may be driving your co-worker
1. _____
2. _____
3. _____
4. _____
5. _____

5) Create two TestIQ based on the above Unmets.
1. _____
_____
_____
_____
_____

2. _____
_____
_____
_____
_____

6) Take a moment to reflect on the importance of Picturing, Articulating, Realizing, and Testing in a PARTNER conversation. Next, fill in the spaces below with reasons why these are important keys in the process of strengthening your communication and relationships (the first one has been filled in for you as an example). Testing is an important step in the process of improving communications and relationship because:

a. They bring the Unmet driving actions to the surface, as such they get to the source of the problem.
b. _____
c. _____
d. _____

_____
_____
_____

KEY FIVE: NUGGET

So far you have explored the "PART" in the PARTNER method. You've used *Picture* to unlock observations and your emanations; *Articulate* to unlock bias free communication; *Realize* to unlock the other person's perspective and EAR listening; and *Test* to help unlock the Unmet(s) by looking behind Shields. In this chapter you will read about the way the "N" fits into the model, and you will learn how the "PART" and the "N" work together. The fifth key of the PARTNER model, the *Nugget* key is about unlocking options.

The goal of the Nugget key is to identify possible options. Nuggets are small but valuable pieces of knowledge or information. Simply put, *a Nugget is a possible option.* To Nugget is to brainstorm alternatives for meeting the Unmet. When PARTNERing you assist the other person in generating Nuggets by focusing your questions on options which can potentially address the identified Unmet. Nuggeting empowers the other person as they brainstorm options to meet their Unmet need(s).

As the other person Nuggets, it is important to remember that there is always more than one suitable option. Nuggeting is about having the other person identify *their* place of greatest potential. There is no right or wrong option—there are no mistakes—just possibilities. Looking at every Nugget, as a viable option for addressing the Unmet, opens up and expands possibility.

The Nuggets for meeting the Unmet come from the other person. Why?—Because the Nugget will become *their* answer, option, or solution. The other person will live with and implement the Nugget. As such it is important to draw potential Nuggets from the other person. Remember, the other person will execute the potential Nugget and make it work in their life. This means that Nuggeting is free from the projection of your own perspectives, assumptions, interpretations, assessments, or solutions.

One way to draw options from the other person is to ask NuggetIQs. The goal of a NuggetIQ is to solicit options from the other person. NuggetIQs generate thinking in others; they inspire creativity, and bring possibility to light. Remember to set an agenda for the NuggetIQ by incorporating the Unmet need into the question. This helps both you and the other person to stay focused. When Nuggeting, engage the other person, and use NuggetIQ's to draw upon multiple sources for inspiration. There are many ways to create a NuggetIQ. Below are examples of NuggetIQ's (questions to uncover options for meeting the Unmet) that can be used to *query* and draw out the other person's perspective. You can generate their thinking by:

Quizzing by asking for options; e.g.: "What would help you with _____ (insert Unmet need)? What would resolve this for you?"

Uncovering options from history; e.g.: "What has worked in the past when _____ (insert Unmet need) was an issue for you?"

Exploring the environment: "What have you seen others do to address _____ (insert Unmet need)?"

Requesting from the future: "If this_____ (insert Unmet) were resolved, what would it look like?" Wait for a description and then ask: "What are the steps you can take to get there?"

Yielding Support: "What can I do to help with addressing _____ (insert Unmet)?" Wait for an answer and then ask: "Where should we start?"

If the other person is unable to come up with options, then you may offer some using an AddIQ. This is not the same as projecting your own solution onto the situation. Rather, you are trying to stimulate thinking in the other person by offering new information. When using an AddIQ the Unmet is used as the agenda, you offer options and you end by inviting the other person to think. An AddIQ is generated by applying the following formula:

AddIQ = Agenda (Unmet) + Offer1 + Offer2 + Invitation

The following are examples of how AddIQs (how they work and what you use them for):

Arousing Collaboration. To address the (insert Unmet) I'll think of one option (offer1) and you think of another (offer2 combined with invitation to think deeper)."

Divulging Personal Experience. "When faced with (insert the Unmet) this option (offer1) has worked for me and this one (offer2) has worked for me as well, what are some other alternatives (invitation)?"

Drawing from the environment. "To address (insert the Unmet) I've seen others do this (offer1) as well as this (offer2). What are other possibilities (invitation for deeper thinking)?"

When you offer, you share knowledge, and you invite the other person to find his or her own path. By inviting the other person to think deeper, you are asking them to clarify, label, unveil and explain options instead of projecting your perception of what possible options are. NuggetIQs and AddIQs both motivate thinking in the other person.

When searching for Nuggets, solicit ideas from the other person first by drawing out their perspective with NuggetIQ's. If the other person is unable to generate options, then you may use AddIQ's where you offer more than one idea to create a range of choices and end with a request asking the person for additional options. Draw from the other person as many options as possible so he or she can select the most promising or appealing idea. By generating multiple possibilities, the other person comes away with a sense of ownership of the outcome. PARTNERing is about respecting other people's ability to choose for their own lives, and supporting them in owning their own empowerment. Keep in mind that Nuggeting involves supporting the other person as they seek options to address the identified Unmet (the driver behind the behavior). Let's practice Nuggeting with some skill builders.

SKILL BUILDER: 1

1) Moral in the company is low— it's time for team building! You have been charged with talking to the team and generating a list of options for meeting the Unmet. First, identify the Unmet that you want to focus on. Two possible Unmets are positive company moral and increased teambuilding, there are others you can use, take a moment to list them below.

_____

_____

_____

_____

_____

_____

2) Choose an Unmet to focus on. Circle it and then create a list of questions you can use with the team as you Nugget for options to address the chosen Unmet. Incorporate as many QUERY questions as you can.

_____

_____

_____

_____

_____

_____

SKILL BUILDER: 2

A meeting has been set up for you to speak with other employees. In this meeting you will be discussing company issues. As morale is low, this meeting is an opportunity for team building and the meeting is being catered. You have been assigned a co-worker to help you arrange the food. Together you must both come up with food options. Use the AddIQs to Nugget for options with your co-worker. Before doing this identify what the Unmet is in this situation. Is it food, or that people enjoy the food, or that there is a variety of food, or what else could the Unmet be? Once you have the Unmet that you want to use identified, use the space below to create a list of AddIQs to generate options.

_____
_____
_____
_____
_____
_____
_____
_____
_____
_____
_____
_____
_____
_____
_____
_____

EMPOWERMENT

Empowerment is a key element of being *person-centered*. What is being person-centered? It's focusing on the other person's needs and not letting your BIAS dominate or override the other person's perspective. As you PARTNER you empower by opening yourself to the understanding that the other person has the best insight into their own lives—they understand their hopes and dreams best; they know their situation, they will live out and follow through with their own decisions. All people are the authority for their own life and can choose what is best for them. As you PARTNER the other person clues you into this as they define their options. Each Nugget that is uncovered empowers the other person. The other person is exercising control over their lives as they clarify, label, unveil and explain the options as they understand them. Through PARTNERing you are empowering the other person and supporting them in doing this. You want them to Nugget and clue into what works for them, without projecting your own solution on to them.

By empowering others to find their own path you AVOID projecting your BIAS. You AVOID BIAS by choosing not to engage in any of the following actions:

Assuring
- Example: "Don't worry; you're overreacting. It will be O.K. Don't let it get to you…"
- Instead: Provide the opportunity for the other person to vent, and then brainstorm Nuggets when the time is right.

Victimizing
- Example: "You shouldn't be reacting this way or……….."
- Instead: Ask questions to understand what is driving the reaction; brainstorm Nuggets.

Ordering
- Example: "Stop this anger, right now!"
- Instead: Provide the other person space to vent. Validate their

emotions and ask questions to understand what is occurring, then Nugget.

Informing

- Example: "You have it all wrong. What is really bothering you is…….. or the problem is…"
- Instead: Ask the other person to tell you what the challenge is. Provide venting time; find the unmet need, then Nugget.

Directing

- Example: "Maybe you should do this…"
- Instead: Ask if you can offer a suggestion, then Nugget more options from the other person.

When you Nugget, the focus is on empowering future possibilities, not highlighting missteps or past errors. However, there are some occasions when bringing up the past can be helpful. When the past is brought up, it is used for assessing and uncovering the strengths and resources the other person has. Let's take a look at an example.

Scenario: Your child is learning how to balance homework. However, assignments are not getting turned in and you are receiving calls from your child's teacher. In the past, he has tried creating a daily routine that incorporates homework time. He has tried carrying around an assignment book to write down the assignments and their due dates. He has also tried using his cell phone to remind him of the assignment due dates a week in advance, but to no avail.

Highlighting missteps: "You tried following a routine, which did not work, then you tried carrying around an assignment book to write down assignments but you forgot this at home most of the time. You even tried to set cell phone reminders which you would read and then ignore. Your homework is never in on time."

Now review the situation by engaging in Nuggeting:

You: "The goal is to get your assignments in on time. What would help with this?"

Kid: "Nothing. It's too difficult, I've tried everything, I hate school. I should just drop out."

You: "The goal is for you to get your assignments in on time. When you created a routine, used an assignment book, or set cell phone reminders, what was helpful? What did you struggle with?"

Kid: "The assignment book was difficult. I had a hard time keeping track of it. I liked having a routine, but it was never written down, so I forgot it. I also liked the cell reminders, but my phone was not someplace where I saw it so it was easy to overlook."

You: "The goal is to get your assignments in on time. You liked having a routine and the cell reminders but they were not convenient in that you could readily find them. Can you think of something to address this?"

Kid: "I did find a routine to be comforting and the days I used it I felt in control and balanced. I also liked having the cell reminders, as they helped me to know what was coming. Maybe if I create a calendar, put it in my room with my assignment due dates on a piece of poster board, and hang it to the back of my door, it might be easier than trying to keep it all in my head."

Nuggeting is about gathering an assortment of possibilities—having the other person clue you into options instead of selecting solutions and projecting them onto the other person. Options are found by exploring strengths. Stay clear of highlighting missteps—pointing the finger at the other person or using blame. Instead, when Nuggeting, discover what worked and what didn't and fine-tune with the other person what has worked in the past. It's time to strengthen your skills in Nuggeting with some more practice!

SKILL BUILDER: 3

Look at the scenarios below. In the circle, identify if the response is Assuring, Victimizing, Ordering, Informing, or Directing.

1) Scenario: David is late for work once again.

   a. "David, what you need to do is catch the bus earlier."

   b. "David, you can't continue to be so irresponsible and be late."

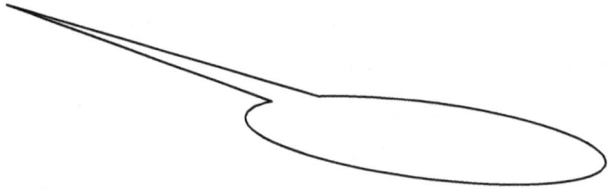

2) Scenario: Your daughter comes into the house crying. After talking with her, you discover it's because she tore her favorite dress.

   a. "Don't be sad, the dress can be replaced."

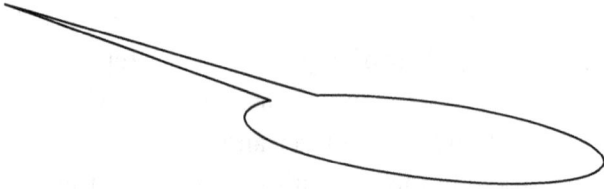

b. "You're not really upset about the dress, you were just embarrassed."

3. "Stop being so upset!"

REFOCUS

Searching for options is never simple. Sometimes the other person's stress can make it difficult for them to generate options. When this happens you might encounter resistance. Expect it, but don't quit PARTNERing. Instead, refocus and try again. Refocusing provides support, by highlighting the strengths the other person has to work through the situation; it can reduce stress for both you and those you PARTNER with.

Just as you reconstruct your stress-inducing MindTalk (dialogue inside your head), when you PARTNER you also refocus the stress-inducing talk of others into encouraging motivating messages. Let's look at an example.

> *Scenario:* A co-worker or child is not able to find options during the Nugget process.
>
> *Stress-Inducing Talk:* "This process is stupid, it's too difficult."
>
> *Refocus to Stress-Reducing Positive Talk:* "I hear this is a challenge for you. I have seen you overcome challenges before. Remember that you figured out how to get to work on time last week. You were able to get through that, even though it was difficult."

The above example of a refocus highlights for the other person the strengths he/she has available to them. While working through a challenging process or task, you encourage the other person by drawing on their strengths and reinforcing this with an example from their past experiences. Notice that the refocus does not contain any promises or false praise. It focused on the underlying Unmet (lack of confidence) that the Shield ("it's stupid") was covering, and it motivated the other person by using an example from their past. In other words, it clued the other person into strengths they missed. Notice that when the past was brought up it was not used for blame, but was used to empower the other person. There are four elements in a refocus called WINS:

Wall — The barrier as the other person perceives it. Unveil the wall and reflect it by incorporating the words of the other person: "I hear this is a challenge for you."

Influence — Nurture by highlighting previous wins or strengths with a factual example: "I've seen you overcome challenges before."

Nudge — Decode resistance by connecting wins and strengths to the barrier: "Remember, last week, you figured out how to get to work on time."

Skill — Use your NuggetIQs to identify what skills helped: "What did you do then that you might be able to do now?"

As you PARTNER, when you hear stress-inducing talk in another, refocus by looking at the WINS and drawing attention to positive, stress-reducing talk.

It's time to put Nuggeting into practice and get ready for the next key with a few skill builders!

SKILL BUILDER: 4

1) In the space below, write a brief overview of a recent decision you made.

_____
_____
_____
_____
_____
_____
_____

2) What was the Unmet?

_____
_____
_____
_____
_____
_____
_____

3) What other options were there? List at least two next to each bullet. Write how the other options would or would not have addressed the Unmet and include the pros and cons as well.

- _____
- _____
- _____
- _____
_____
_____
_____

SKILL BUILDER: 5

1) Refer back to page 93, (the list of unmets that need addressing in your life). In the space below Nugget for options to: address the unmet (you can refer back to the NuggetIQs on pages 114 and 115 to generate thinking).

_____
_____
_____
_____
_____
_____
_____
_____
_____

2) Refer back to page 107, (the list of Shields that you use to cover the unmet). In the space below Nugget for options to communicate your unmet instead of covering it with a shield.

_____
_____
_____
_____
_____
_____
_____
_____
_____

3) Using the scale below circle the number that identifies where you are on the scale when it comes to finding more than one possible option (nugget).

Never   Always
  1   2   3   4   5   6   7   8   9   10

2) If your score was not a 10, then generate Nuggets, for finding more than one option (what steps can you take to move yourself up one point along the spectrum?).

_____
_____
_____
_____
_____
_____
_____
_____

SKILL BUILDER: 6

Before moving onto the next key let's take a moment to practice Picturing, Articulation, Realizing, Testing, and Nuggeting. Remember, when you Picture you observe neutrally and when you Articulate you put your observations into words. When you Realize you unlock the barrier as the other person sees it, when you Test you uncover the Unmet and when you Nugget you unlock options. Let's apply these skills to a specific scenario.

1) You have gone on a camping trip with a friend. After unpacking the car you both notice that the tent was forgotten. This weekend is about bonding with your friend and spending time together. Which of the following statements incorporates the PARTN?

   a. "I noticed we forgot the tent."
   b. "What made you forget the tent?"
   c. "We were supposed to have fun this weekend, I can't see any way this is possible now. Are you in agreement that we are out of options?"
   d. "I noticed we forgot the tent. Our goal this weekend was to spend time together, what can we do to have shelter for the night?"
   e. "We drove out here to camp and we forgot the tent. Our goal is to have bonding time. What are our options for spending time together?"

2) Take a moment to reflect on the importance of Picturing, Articulating, Realizing, Testing, and Nuggeting in a PARTNER conversation. Next, fill in the spaces below with reasons why these are important keys in the process of strengthening your communication and relationships (the first one has been filled in for you as an example). Nuggeting is an important step in the process of improving communications and relationship because:

a. It brings to light multiple options
b.
c.
d.

Key Six: Evaluate

So far you have explored the "PARTN" in the PARTNER method. *Picture* was the first key, it was applied to observations and used to unlock ways to RELEASE. *Articulate* was second, and was applied to putting observations into words and used to unlock the Domino Cycle. Third came *Realize*, this was used to uncover the barrier and to help unlock IQs. *Test* was fourth, this key was used to look at what was behind the barrier—it was used to unlock the Unmet. Fifth was *Nugget*, this was used to uncover options and unlock WINS. Now you will be using the sixth key—*Evaluate*. This key will unlock next steps. *When Evaluating your goal is twofold: 1) to facilitate the ability to choose the Next Strategy, and 2) to create a plan that includes a way to implement the chosen strategy and a Back-Up Strategy.*

The Next Strategy

Facilitating the other person's ability to choose the Next Strategy is accomplished by empowering the other person as they choose from the available Nuggets and by supporting the chosen Nugget (option)—whether you agree with the option or not.

Choosing the next strategy is like putting a floral arrangement together. There is no single "right" way to make a floral arrangement. There are many options, many ways to create an arrangement. When choosing the next strategy the other person looks at the Nuggets and chooses a Nugget or an arrangement of Nuggets that meet their unmet need(s). The onus is on the other person to assess the Nuggets and choose which to implement. Your role is to organize the Nuggets and this is accomplished with EvaluateIQs.

When you ask EvaluateIQs you are empowering the other person to create an arrangement that addresses their Unmet needs. EvaluateIQs facilitate the other person's ability to clarify and unveil their next steps. It is important that you resist creating their arrangement—keep bias out of your EvaluateIQ's. This means you refrain from asking questions like "This is the solution you should go with, don't you agree?" or using statement like, "What you should do is..."—EvaluateIQs do not include your selection of the other person's next step. Instead you seek from the other person the next strategy they want. When you use an EvaluateIQ you are in essence asking the other person: "What do you want to try?" A possible script for an EvaluateIQ that asks the other person about the next strategy is:

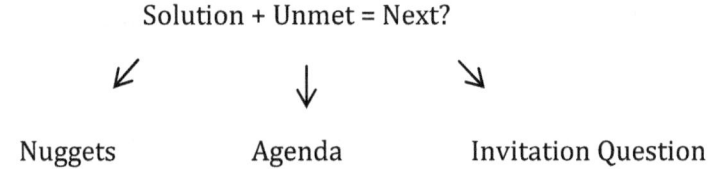

Solution + Unmet = Next?

Nuggets   Agenda   Invitation Question

The script is enacted by using the following EvaluateIQ formula:

"These were the options (Nuggets) here is what the unmet they address (agenda), which works best for you (invitation to choose the next step)?"

Let's explore this with an example. It's time for your best friend to buy a new family car. Your friend did not have a car before, but, having moved recently, getting a car is now unavoidable. She has been looking around and has found several options: a convertible, a minivan, a truck with or without an extended cab, a sport utility, and a sedan. In addition she has discovered electric cars, cars that run on gasoline and cars that run on bio-diesel. She is also looking at new verses used cars. In short, your friend has many options and many decisions to make.

She plans to use the car, daily to take the kids to school, and weekly to run errands like grocery shopping. In addition, she wants to use it for family vacations (camping trips in the spring and fall, trips to the mountains to ski in the winter and trips to the beach in the summer). You are out car shopping with her. You're not the one picking the car, but you are there to support her. Her primary Unmet is having an affordable vehicle to take the kids to school. So you ask an EvaluateIQ:

"These were the options: a convertible, a minivan, a truck with or without an extended cab, a sport utility, and a sedan (list of Nuggets). You said that you need a car primarily for taking the kids to and from school (Unmet), what works best to fit your primary need (next strategy)?

Although this may seem simple, it is not. Sometimes it requires more than just asking what will meet the Unmet, at times it may be necessary to use evaluation criteria to narrow/arrange the Nuggets. Evaluation criteria take many forms, however they always serve as a measuring point to help the other person decide between Nuggets (options). Below are some options for finding a POINT of measure (the criteria below are not the only evaluation criteria, they are meant to generate thinking). When evaluating Nuggets it might be helpful to look at and assess:

Profit/Loss—The gains and losses associated with a particular choice.

Order—Rate the options on a scale ranging from one to ten.

Issues—Look at a list of outcomes that the option needs to address and check off the issues that the option addresses, then add up check marks at the end.

Needs—Look at what is needed to implement a Nugget, assess whether the resources are available. Hypothetical situations can be used to help with this.

Tactic—Examine whether a nugget will or will not work and the reasons why.

Evaluation criteria provide a way for the other person to organize and assess the Nuggets. Remember that not every Nugget will address all the criteria, but by utilizing criteria you have a standard by which to Evaluate the Nuggets. Let's go back to the car example. There are so many options available, and your friend feels lost. You PARTNER with her to assess her options by looking at any of the following POINTs (it is not necessary to use all the evaluation criteria listed below, choose what fits the situation and use it):

Profit/Loss—The gains and losses associated with a particular choice.
- What would she give up to afford each kind of car? What would she benefit from each?

Order—Rate the options on a scale ranging from one to ten.
- How does she rank the options, based on what she likes?

Issues—Look at a list of outcomes that the option needs to address, check off the issues that the option addresses, then you add up check marks at the end.
- What are the features of the car, its functionality, and how does it serve its purpose in her family?

Needs—Look at what is needed to implement a Nugget, assess whether the resources are available. Hypothetical situations can be used to help with this.
- What is the cost of financing, cost of ownership etcetera and her resources?

Tactic—Examine whether a Nugget will or will not work and the reasons why.

- Eliminate the options she does not like, then look at the ones that are left.

The above examples demonstrated different ways to Evaluate—they are points of measurement for assessing the Nuggets that are available to address the Unmet. Having assessed the options with your friend ask the EvaluateIQ (question to choose the next strategy) again by saying: "These were the options (list of cars), this is what was being addressed (transport to take the kids to school), based on your assessment, what works best (next)?"

When the next strategy is chosen it's time to work on a PLAN to implement the chosen strategy and a back-up strategy.

THE PLAN

The PLAN has two parts: 1) the concrete steps for executing the chosen strategy, and 2) a back-up or alternative to the chosen strategy. A PLAN can cover:

Purpose—Which option will be used (the selected nugget) and why (the unmet it addresses).

Length—When will it be done - time frame for executing the Nugget and/or reviewing the effectiveness.

Alternatives—How will obstacles be handled - planning ahead of time, how to overcome obstacles.

Navigation—What will be done - what will be needed, and the steps for carrying it out.

Creating a strong PLAN is necessary for the option (Nugget) to become a successful strategy.

CONCRETE ACTION PLAN

A concrete action plan involves helping others clue into and think through the process of executing their choice. This is where potential blocks are identified—those issues that might get in the way of the PLAN. Formulating a concrete plan requires addressing how blocks might be overcome. This involves being realistic and specific with the chosen path—what will happen, when, and how—it requires planning. You focus IQs (invitation/open questions) on the specific details. This might include Who, What, Where, When, and How. Examples include:

- What are you going to do?
- Who are you going to do it with?
- How are you going to do it?
- When are you going to do it?
- What do you need to accomplish the task?

These questions break the chosen strategy down into small detailed steps. Realistic, specific plans empower the other person. Being concrete supports the other person as they prepare to and carry out the strategy they have chosen. Remember, the other person clarifies and unveils a concrete plan that they can follow through with. As you PARTNER with the other person, refrain from projecting your assessment of what a concrete plan is. Below is an example of concrete planning using specific details.

Scenario: Your child decides he will bake a cake for dessert on Friday. As part of planning you ask the following:

Parent: "How long will it take to bake the cake?"
Kid: "It usually takes about an hour."
Parent: "It's Monday. When will you have an hour to bake the cake for Friday?"
Kid: "Wednesday evening after school, since I have no after school activities."

Parent: "Around what time?"
Kid: "At 5."
Parent: "What do you need to do to get prepared?"
Kid: "Make sure I have all the ingredients."
Parent: "When do you have time for that?"
Kid: "Tonight will be good. I'm going to bed at 8:30, so if I review the recipe at 8. I can see if we have all the ingredients."
Parent: "What will you do if you don't have everything you need?"
Kid: "I will write it down."
Parent: "How will you get the missing ingredients?"
Kid: "I will ask you to take me to the grocery store on the way home tomorrow."
Parent: "You're baking a cake on Friday. Tonight, before bedtime, you will review the recipe. If you are missing any ingredients, you will write them down. Where will you put the list?"
Kid: "I will put it on the fridge."
Parent: "On Tuesday after school we will pick up any missing ingredients. Then Wednesday around 5 you will bake the cake. Is there anything else you need to do to get ready?"
Kid: "No, I have the pans and a cake plate. And, when I bake it, I will put it in the fridge with a note labeling it as dessert for dinner on Friday."
Parent: "Sounds like a plan."

As the above example shows, creating a concrete plan involves being specific, and incorporates the other person's perspective. The other person clarifies and explains what they will do and when. Let's take a moment to practice these skills.

SKILL BUILDER: 1

Morale in the company is low. It's time for team building. You have been charged with talking to the team and generating a list of options for meeting the Unmet. The Unmet that you are trying to address is low morale. Possible options are to hold a company picnic, take the team on a weekend retreat, plan weekly lunch meetings outside the office for bonding, or bring in a facilitator to help the team hash out issues. After discussing the Evaluate IQ, it's been decided that there will be a company picnic. In the space below create a list of questions that you might ask to create a concrete plan for making the company picnic happen.

_____

_____

_____

_____

_____

_____

EAR LISTENING AND HEARING

It is important to use your EAR to listen so that you can HEAR the other person. When using EAR listening, support the other person as they clarify, label, unveil, and explain themselves and their perspective. Refrain from letting BIAS cloud what you hear. As you use, EAR listening it's helpful to know what you are listening for, remember to pay attention so you HEAR the information you receive from the other person. This means you listen for their:

Handle: Their perception and judgment on things; the truth as they see it, their reality.

Elicitation: What they request, what they want; the Unmet need.

Advantage: The skills and strengths they have; the options, what they are able to do, their strengths.

Resolve: What will they do.

Let's clarify this with an example:

"John is harassing me (Handle). He just hits me for no good reason (Handle). It makes me nervous to be around him (Elicitation — request for safety). I will hit him next time (Resolve)."

When you PARTNER, it is important to really use EAR listening and HEAR how and what the other person is conveying—the clues they send. This helps you to gain insight.

BACK-UP PLAN

When Evaluating, it is also important to have a *Back-Up Plan*. A Back-Up Plan is the contingency arrangement that the other person will defer to if the Next Strategy does not address the Unmet. In creating a Back-Up Plan, simply ask: "What is your Plan B?" When you PARTNER with the other person to create a Back-Up Plan, refrain from telling the other person what the back-up *should* be. If the other person does not select the option you are comfortable with for their primary plan, refrain from saying things such as: "If the plan you choose does not work, then I suggest you..." Remember when you PARTNER with the other person they lead the way, as such they choose the Back-Up Plan. Now it's your turn to put this into practice and build your skills!

SKILL BUILDER: 2

Look at the skit below and in the box identify what you HEAR (handle, elicitation, advantage, resolve) being used by the other person.

Co-worker: "This project will never get done."

↖ [   ]

You: "Let me see if I understand; you believe this project will never get done. What is causing you to believe this?"

Co-worker: "I've been working on it for months and every time I turn around there is something new or a new problem; it's just so very frustrating!"

↖ [   ]

You: "So you're frustrated right now. Do you need help with the project or a break or what else?"

Co-worker: "I need support."

↖ [   ]

You: "If you had support, how would the project progress differently?"

Co-worker: "Things would be organized."

↖ [   ]

You "What has helped in the past with other projects in which you felt organized?"

Co-worker: "Talking with my boss and getting feedback, having a schedule of deadlines, and knowing who I could ask for help."

↖ [   ]

You: "So you're frustrated; this project seems to be taking a long time; and you need support with being more organized. In the past, feedback has helped you stay organized, along with having a schedule and knowing who to ask for help. Which of these will help with this project?"

Co-worker: "I guess I can ask my boss to check in with me and do a daily debrief for this project."

You: "When will you speak with your boss?"
Co-worker: "I will do it first thing tomorrow."

You: "And what if he has no time in the morning?"
Co-worker: "I will e-mail him."

You: "What's another option you might try?"
Co-worker: "If my boss is unavailable, I will create a schedule of deadlines and send it to him."

You: "You were feeling frustrated but, after we talked for a bit, you found options that would help you feel organized. Thank you for taking the time to discuss this with me."

SKILL BUILDER: 3

1) What are some questions you can use to create a Back-Up Plan for the company picnic?

_____
_____
_____
_____
_____
_____
_____
_____
_____
_____
_____
_____
_____
_____
_____

SKILL BUILDER: 4

To help you understand the Evaluate key, take a moment to put it into practice in your own life. Fill in the following:

1) A decision I'm contemplating is:

_____
_____
_____
_____

2) The possible options are (list at least 3):

_____
_____
_____
_____

3) The need is:

_____
_____
_____
_____

4) I can evaluate the options using the following criterion:

_____
_____
_____
_____

5) The option that matches the need best is:

_____
_____
_____
_____

6) The steps I need to take to implement the option are (list at least 3 steps in sequence, including a date and time deadline for implementation). Include: What will be done. When it will be done. How you plan to do it.

_____
_____
_____
_____

7) I can be held accountable for following through with my decision by:

_____
_____
_____
_____

SKILL BUILDER: 5

1) Write something that you plan to achieve in the next six months.

_____
_____
_____
_____

2) In the space below, describe how your life will be different as a result of this; describe the future.

_____
_____
_____
_____

3) Look at your description and write at least three steps you will need to take to get from where you are to the future.

_____
_____
_____
_____

4) Pick one step and write how you will achieve it, what you need to do, the time you need, and how you will know when you have achieved this step.

_____
_____
_____
_____

5) Write all the reasons why achieving this goal is important.

_____
_____
_____
_____
_____

6) Turn your reasons into empowering motivating statements (EMS see pg. 49) below.

_____
_____
_____
_____
_____

7) In the space below, list any potential blocks.

_____
_____
_____
_____
_____

8) Pick three blocks and write how you will overcome them. Include the empowering motivating statements you created.

_____
_____
_____
_____
_____

SKILL BUILDER: 6

Before moving onto the next key let's take a moment to practice Picturing, Articulation, Realizing, Testing, Nuggeting, and Evaluating. Remember when you Picture you observe neutrally and when you Articulate you put your observations into words. When you Realize you unlock the barrier as the other person sees it, when you Test you uncover the Unmet. When you Nugget you unlock options and when you Evaluate you unlock next steps. Let's apply these skills to a specific scenario.

1) You have gone on a camping trip with a friend. After unpacking the car you both notice that the tent was forgotten. This weekend is about bonding with your friend and spending time together. You and your friend explore options to meet the Unmet which was time together: you could go back home for the tent, stay at a nice hotel for the weekend, or go back to town, have dinner tonight and go golfing tomorrow, then fishing the next day. Which of the following incorporates the PARTNE?

   a. "We drove out here to camp and we forgot the tent. Our goal is to have bonding time — we can either drive back and get the tent, spend the weekend at a resort, or head home and go golfing. Which of these gives us the most bonding time?"
   b. "If we drive back and it's too dark to come back to the campsite, what will our back up plan be?"
   c. Both A and B
   d. "I noticed we forgot the tent. Let's go home."
   e. "We can just hang out another weekend."
   f. "Did we have a Back-Up Plan?"
   g. "This is not how the weekend was supposed to be."

2) Take a moment to reflect on the importance of Picturing, Articulating, Realizing, Testing, Nuggeting, and Evaluating in a PARTNER conversation. Next, fill in the spaces below with reasons why these are important keys in the process of strengthening your

communication and relationships (the first one has been filled in for you as an example). Evaluating is an important step in the process of improving communications and relationship because:

a. It helps move the process forward toward action.
b.
c.
d.

Key Seven: Reinforce

It's time to use the final key, *Reinforce*. First, let's review the six keys leading to the final stage in the PARTNER process. You began with *Picture* where you observed and unlocked Reconstructing. The second key was *Articulate* which helped with putting observations into words; it was also used to unlock the ability to neutralize. The third key, *Realize*, helped to identify the barrier and you learned how to Take Five. Next was key four, *Test*, which involved connecting to what was behind the barrier. This was followed by the fifth key, *Nugget,* which was used to unlock options by QUERYing from sources. Evaluate was the sixth key and it was used to unlock next steps. Now it's time to apply the seventh and final key, Reinforce.

The Reinforce key unlocks feedback and empowerment. The process of feedback and empowerment covers all that was done during PARTNERing. To Reinforce is to review and validate a person's efforts, it provides feedback on what was done and acknowledges the efforts of other people by thanking them for their diligence. *It focuses on the process, not the outcome.* This means:

- Recapping what took place
- Highlighting strengths
- Reviewing wins

Reinforcing occurs immediately, without applying any judgment adjectives such as "good job" or "great effort." Again, you don't want to apply BIAS to this process. Instead, you highlight the wins, using gratitude and, by giving attention to someone's strengths. Here is an example:

> *Judgment-based Validation (BIAS):* "You did a good job (judgment) cleaning up after yourself today. I'm proud of you (judgment)."

> *Reinforcement Validation:* "I noticed you put away the bread and meat after you made a sandwich. I also saw you wipe down the counter (specific and fact-based). Thank you for doing that (appreciation)."

Now let's build your Reinforcement skills with some practice!

SKILL BUILDER: 1

The PARTNER model encourages you to validate others, but validation can also be applied to self. It is important for you to validate your own journey in addition to validating the attempts of others.

Take a moment to practice validating yourself. Think about the gifts and traits you bring to your job and family every day and turn them into empowering motivating statements (EMS see pg. 49).

- *I am patient.*
-
-
-
-
-
-
-
-

SKILL BUILDER: 2

It is important to celebrate the successes of others and ourselves. Fill in the blanks below to build Self-Reinforcement.

1) My best trait is:

_____
_____

2) I feel positively about myself for:

_____
_____

3) Every day I do the following to rejuvenate:

_____
_____

4) Within the last 24 hours, I did the following well:

_____
_____

5) During the last 24 hours, I rewarded myself by:

_____
_____

6) From now on, I commit to noticing my successes and rewarding or reinforcing myself by:

_____
_____

SKILL BUILDER: 3

Let's take a moment to practice Picturing, Articulation, Realizing, Testing, Nuggeting, Evaluating and Reinforcement. Remember the PARTNER steps. When you: Picture you observe neutrally; Articulate you put your observations into words; Realize you unlock the barrier as the other person sees it; Test you uncover the Unmet; Nugget you unlock options; Evaluate you unlock next steps, and Reinforce you unlock feedback and empowerment. Use the following example to apply all seven PARTNER keys.

1) You have gone on a camping trip with a friend. After unpacking the car you both notice that the tent was forgotten. This weekend is about bonding with your friend and spending time together. You and your friend explored options to meet the Unmet (which was spending time together). Together you chose that tonight you will go out for a nice dinner and return to town, go golfing tomorrow and, the day after go fishing. Which of the following incorporates the PARTNER?

    a.   "We drove out here to camp and we forgot the tent. Our goal is to have bonding time."
    b.   "We decided to go home."
    c.   "We drove out here to camp and we forgot the tent. Our goal is to have bonding time. We took some time to come up with options and choose to go home tonight, then go golfing tomorrow, and, if we are not too tired, fishing the next day. Thanks for taking the time to talk this out with me."

2) Take a moment to reflect on the importance of Picturing, Articulating, Realizing, Testing, Nuggeting, Evaluating, and Reinforcing in a PARTNER conversation. Next, list reasons why these are important keys in the process of strengthening your communication and relationships (the first one has been filled in for you as an example). Reinforcement is an important step in the process of improving communications and relationship because:

a.   *It highlights the positives and this generates goodwill.*
b.
c.
d.
e.
f.

Conclusion
The Seven Partner Keys

What an exciting, enlightening journey! The PARTNER model is now yours—it belongs to you. You have the keys you need to identify and aid in bringing out the strengths in others. Use them to unlock greater harmony in your life and relationships. I invite you to practice the PARTNER keys—individually and collectively. You have learned how to use the PARTNER keys to unlock your conversations. You know how to *Picture, Articulate, Realize, Test, Nugget, Evaluate and Reinforce!*

Let's take a moment to recap what you have learned. The goal of the PARTNER model is to learn how to clue into and use the other person's perspective. To support your ability to do this, you learned how to refrain from BIAS by tapping into your BodyTalk (sensations in your body)—clueing you into the signals of high stress. You learned to assess MindTalk (dialogue in your head) and to Reconstruct reactionary thinking by using the GIFT (grow, improve, find, transition) principle. To support your ability to use the GIFT principle, you learned RELEASE (defusing high-stress) techniques, and about using EMS (Encouraging Motivational Statements). Remember, you want to use your influence positively, as a PLUS, instead of negatively to PICK.

You learned about using Invitation Questions (IQs) to open a space for the other person to share their perspective. You discovered how to benefit from EAR listening so that you HEAR deeply what is being communicated. You practiced how to AVOID actions that inhibit your ability to empower and accept the other person. In short you figured out how to PARTNER.

PARTNERing is focused on strengths, developed via communication, balanced by promoting wellness and wholeness, and continually moving forward by validating successes. PARTNER conversations create a safe space for the other person to open up and share because PARTNERing is bias free—discards judgment, criticism and assumption. Instead PARTNERing is open and creative—knowing the answer is within the other person.

Understanding, learning, and practicing PARTNERing will help you to expand the lines of communication between yourself and those you are in relationship with. Your relationships will strengthen. Remember as you PARTNER, you engage in a new kind of dialogue. Your conversations are about support, empowerment, and acceptance. As you move forward and make the model your own remember to focus on using the seven keys in PARTNER conversations:

P *Picture*: unlocks observations

A *Articulate*: unlocks words

R *Realize*: unlocks barriers

T *Test*: unlocks the unmet need or unspoken desire behind the barrier

N *Nugget*: unlocks possible options

E *Evaluate*: unlocks next steps

R *Reinforce*: unlocks feedback and empowerment

Now that you have learned how to use the seven PARTNER keys you will find that by applying the PARTNER model to conversations you emerge as a support figure in the lives of those around you. The PARTNER keys help increase the flexibility and creativity in your relationship with others. It expands openness and spurs the willingness to explore new possibilities. As you continue to practice PARTNERing you will see changes in yourself and your relationships.

As you PARTNER honor the philosophy of operating without BIAS. You do this by accepting others and controlling yourself. While you learn don't get lost focusing on technical execution, instead focus more on adhering to the essence. As you do you will derive great benefit.

By reconstructing your MindTalk (dialogue in your head), tapping into your BodyTalk (sensations in your body) and using RELEASE strategies you will grow in self-awareness. This will help you to become more skilled at taking accountability for yourself and your actions. As you approach others from a place of curiosity and focus on information gathering, you will find that others become more skilled at taking ownership and accountability for their actions.

PARTNERing is not like medication, it does not cure relationships. PARTNERing develops connection and increases accountability. As you practice know that this is a tool, it is one of many that you can use to build your relationships. When you PARTNER take care not to use the process as a way to fix another person or as a way to get the other person to change. PARTNERing is about drawing out information and options, then freeing yourself so that the other person can take their own individual journey. As you PARTNER, take responsibility for working on your thinking and release the other person to do the same.

Remember, the PARTNER keys guide you easily, yet effectively, on how to create stronger relationship by using your conversations to: unearth information, seek options and build rapport.

Here are a few skill builders to help you practice PARTNERing!

SKILL BUILDER:1

Forming healthy partnerships requires the following values:

| *patience* |
| *acceptance* |
| *resourcefulness* |
| *trustworthiness* |
| *neutrality* |
| *empathy* |
| *reliability* |

Look at the list above, choose your top three (you can include values not on the list), and record them below. Next to each, write an example of a time when you demonstrated it.

1.

2.

3.

SKILL BUILDER: 2

Circle the answer that best reflects the PARTNER philosophy.

Scenario: This is the third time this week that an employee has come to work late. The other members on the team are getting upset.

Which of the following incorporates **Picture** and **Articulate**?
  a. "You are always late."
  b. "You have been late three times this week."
  c. "Your tardiness is an issue."
  d. "You are taking your job for granted."

Which of the following incorporates **Realize**?
  a. "Tell me what's been happening."
  b. "What are you going to do to be on time?"
  c. "If you are late again, I will have to write you up."
  d. "You have been late and you know the team needs you."

Scenario: Your co-worker explains that he is late because he was recently separated from his spouse, the car broke down, and he is having a hard time balancing his life.

Which of the following incorporates **Test**?
  a. "You need to arrange a carpool with your co-workers."
  b. "You need to talk to your ex."
  c. "Am I hearing you say you need help organizing, or getting to work; or, what else is it?"
  d. "You understand that your personal life should not affect your attendance."

Which of the following incorporates **Nugget**?
  a. "What has helped you balance in the past?"
  b. "Tell me why you are the only one who can't balance your work and personal life?"

    c.   "I don't want your excuses; maybe you need time off."
    d.   "Tell me why I shouldn't fire you."

Scenario: Your co-worker has come up with the following options: taking a few days off to get organized, calling a grandparent to help, or talking to their ex about a schedule.

Which of the following incorporates **Evaluate**?
    a.   "What option would you like to try first?"
    b.   "What will you do as a back-up plan?"
    c.   A and B.
    d.   None of the above.

Which of the following incorporates **Reinforce**?
    a.   "Good job."
    b.   "I believe you will be on time from now on."
    c.   "Thank you for sharing and for discussing what you can do differently tomorrow to be on time."
    d.   None of the above.

Answer key available at www.partner-cmd.com.

Unlocking the Power of Words

SKILL BUILDER: 3

Circle the answer that matches the PARTNER philosophy.

Scenario: Your kid leaves his room in a mess yet again.

Which of the following incorporates **Picture** and **Articulate**?
   a.   "As usual, your room is in a mess."
   b.   "Must I do everything?"
   c.   "You told me you would clean your room yesterday and I noticed it's still in need of cleaning."
   d.   "You are a messy child."

Which of the following incorporates **Realize**?
   a.   "As usual, your room is in a mess. Tell me why you don't listen."
   b.   "How many times must I tell you to clean your room?"
   c.   "You told me you would clean your room yesterday and I noticed it's still in need of cleaning. What happened?"
   d.   "You are a messy child. Why is that?"

Which of the following incorporates **Test**?
   a.   "What can I do in order for you to take responsibility?"
   b.   "Do you need me to do it with you, or do you need help organizing your schedule? Or what else might it be?"
   c.   "Tell me what your problem is."
   d.   "How can I get you to show some responsibility?"

Which of the following incorporates **Nugget**?
   a.   "Last week you cleaned your room when you said you would. What helped you with doing that?"
   b.   "Tell me what I should do the next time you don't follow through."
   c.   "How can I help you with this?"
   d.   A and C.

Which of the following incorporates **Evaluate**?
- a. "If you clean your room, we can go out and do something fun."
- b. "If you clean your room, I won't yell at you."
- c. You talked about option A, B, and C. Which do you like best?"
- d. None of the above.

Which of the following incorporates **Reinforce**?
- a. "I'm proud of you."
- b. "You know how to be a good kid."
- c. "We talked about cleaning your room, we discussed what has helped you in the past, and then talked about what you will try in the future. I appreciate your willingness to talk this over."
- d. None of the above.

Answer key available at www.partner-cmd.com.

Unlocking the Power of Words

SKILL BUILDER: 4

Circle the answer that matches the PARTNER philosophy.

Scenario: Your best friend has a hard time committing to anything. Out of the blue, your friend tells you he wants to adopt a kid.

Which of the following incorporates **Picture** and **Articulate**?
    a.   "You want to adopt a kid; that's a big responsibility."
    b.   "Why do you want a kid?"
    c.   "Can you afford to have a child?"
    d.   "I heard you say you're thinking of adopting."

Which of the following incorporates **Realize**?
    a.   "I heard you want a kid; tell me how you're going to be able to do this."
    b.   "I heard you say you're thinking of adopting; tell me more."
    c.   "Why do you want a kid when you work crazy hours?"
    d.   "Who has told you that having a kid will make you happy?"

Scenario: As you PARTNER, you discover that your best friend feels lonely and wants a kid for companionship.

Which of the following incorporates **Test**?
    a.   "So I heard you say that you want to adopt a kid because you need companionship?"
    b.   "If you want a companion, why not get a dog?"
    c.   "Kids are around all the time; if you adopt one, you'll be longing for free time."
    d.   "You can get a dog, or a plant, or come over for dinner more often. Which do you think will help address the need for companionship?"

Which of the following incorporates **Nugget**?
    a.   "If you could paint the perfect future in which you had

companionship, what would that look like?"
b. "What has helped in the past when you needed companionship?"
c. "What have you seen others do when they need companionship?"
d. All of the above.

Which of the following incorporates **Evaluate**?
a. "You need companionship, and we talked about what has helped in the past. Which route would do you think you'd like to take?"
b. "I'm glad you have other options than adopting."
c. "You need to rule out the option of adopting."
d. "I still think you need a dog."

Which of the following incorporates **Reinforce**?
a. "You dodged a bullet."
b. "Thank you for sharing with me."
c. "You mentioned you wanted to adopt a kid. You had a bad suggestion for adopting, and then I told you to get a dog. I'm really glad you listened to me."
d. All of the above

Answer key available at www.partner-cmd.com.

Optional Hidden Bonus
Key Eight: Span

Consider the "S" a hidden key, a bonus. When you add an "S" to the word PARTNER you get PARTNERS. In this guide the PARTNER model has been used to draw out the other person's perspective. This is the premise for PARNTERing—drawing out the other person. Sometimes it may be necessary to add some focus on "self" (the "S" in PARTNERing). This is where the hidden "S" comes into play. Notice, however, that the hidden S works *with* the PARTNER model, it does not override it. PARTNER comes before you add the S.

As you PARTNER, observe yourself, what you say, and how you say it. During this process you may notice that you need to make a request. This is when you add the hidden "S." You use it to make a request, which you might do when you need help or support from those around you, whether at home or at work. When asking for help, it is important to remember to use the PARTNER philosophies you learned. You can do this by using a SpanIQ.

SpanIQ's cannot be answered with a "Yes" or "No," they are an open invitation. When using a SpanIQ, you state:

Specifics – Facts only

Passion – Joint unmet need

Admission – Agenda (link facts to Unmet) and nurture (build a bridge as to why this matters to you and the other person)

Need – Invitation and offering of options

Let's apply the SpanIQ to a specific example. You and your spouse both work a 40-plus-hour week. You have a child and you are both trying to balance your home and work lives. Every week it seems that you become more and more frustrated because your spouse is able to relax while you care for the house and the child. For example, laundry, grocery shopping and house cleaning all need to be done this weekend. However, it's been a long week and you and your spouse both need to relax. Using a SpanIQ, you would say: "This weekend there is laundry, grocery shopping, and house cleaning to do (specifics), and we both need time to unwind (passion). Since taking care of the house and unwinding is important for both of us (admission), which of these would you like to take care of (need)?"

If the above example involved making a request to your kids instead of a spouse you could use a SpanIQ in the following manner: "This weekend there is laundry, grocery shopping and house cleaning to do (specifics), and we all have weekend plans (passion). Since caring for the house and having time for friends is important to all of us (admission), I will do the grocery shopping. So which of the others – laundry or house cleaning – would you like to take care of (need/options)?

By using SpanIQs, requests are made using the Unmet that connects you to the other person. *SpanIQs invite the other person to engage with you.* They can be used with or independently of PARTNER conversations.

Another way to incorporate the "S" self is by engaging in Self-study and being a reflective partner. Reflection helps you span the learning gap.

BEING A REFLECTIVE PARTNER

Being a Reflective PARTNER is important since your personal development and improvement occur by reflecting on your PARTNER interactions as well as by analyzing what went well and what could be improved the next time. Self-Study is part of the reflection process. With Self-Study, you take the time to reflect on your skills, assess your strengths, and build upon them. You can do the Self-Study segments on your own or you may engage a debriefing buddy. A debriefing buddy can listen, offer feedback and provide encouragement.

Now get ready for your final set of skill builders.

SKILL BUILDER: 1

Complete the following.

1) As I use the PARTNER model, the three benefits I see are:
1. _____
2. _____
3. _____
_____

Declaration: I will remind myself of the above benefits to keep me motivated to PARTNER.

2) Three strengths I have that will help me when PARTNERing are:
1. _____
2. _____
3. _____
_____

3) A strength I need more work in developing is:
_____
_____
_____
_____
_____

4) The steps I will take to develop this strength are (describe each step in detail):

Step 1: _____
_____
_____

Step 2:

Step 3:

5) I will know that I have developed this strength because I will be more skilled in:

SKILL BUILDER: 2

Reflect on your most recent interaction with the PARTNER model. Then complete the sentences below and discuss with a debriefing buddy.

1) I did the following well:

_____
_____
_____
_____

2) I would have liked to do this differently:

_____
_____
_____
_____

3) Moving forward, I need to practice this:

_____
_____
_____
_____

4) One small improvement I will work on is:

_____
_____
_____
_____

Congratulations on completing the PARTNER journey! You did it! You have arrived at a new destination in life with a powerful new toolbox you can use to enhance your conversations and relationships. You have now learned how to use the PARTNER keys to unlock your conversations. Now that you have explored the 7 keys and the hidden 8th key of the PARTNER process, you know how to *Picture, Articulate, Realize, Test, Nugget, Evaluate, Reinforce and Span!* However, the journey doesn't end here. You can continue to PARTNER with me through the web site at www.partner-cmd.com where you can submit your comments, questions and stories about how PARTNERing is working for you. I look forward to hearing your feedback and continuing to PARTNER with you.

Glossary

Analytical Listening: to listen to the other person with your head
Articulate: to put observations into words
Bond: to build engagement and invite the other person to share
BodyTalk: the sensations in your body
Emanations: actions, behaviors or moods
Empowerment: when other people have the best insight into their lives
Empathy: compassion, consideration and sensitivity
Evaluate: to empower other people to choose their next step
Exclusive Listening: to listen from your point of view
IQ (Invitation Question): one that cannot be answered with a simple "yes" or "no"
MindTalk: the dialogue that goes on inside your head
Neutrality: relaying your observations without BIAS
Nugget: to brainstorm for ideas on alternatives for meeting the Unmet
Picture: to observe events and take in information
P = P: the tendency to make the person the problem (Person=Problem)
Realize: to have the other person identify the barrier he or she faces
RealizeIQ: to find out "why" something is occurring
Reconstructing: the process by which you replace your thoughts
Reinforce: to validate and provide feedback
Relational Listening: to listen from the other person's point of view

Shield: what the other person presents you with as a statement, behavior, action or option

Test: to connect to what is behind the barrier; recognize/clarify the unmet need or unspoken desire behind the barrier

Unmets: the motivators behind behavior

PARTNER

- **P**   *Picture*: unlocks observations
- **A**   *Articulate*: unlocks words
- **R**   *Realize*: unlocks barriers
- **T**   *Test*: unlocks the unmet need or unspoken desire behind the barrier
- **N**   *Nugget*: unlocks possible options
- **E**   *Evaluate*: unlocks next steps
- **R**   *Reinforce*: unlocks feedback and empowerment

RELEASE TECHNIQUE:

Repeat the alphabet softly or count to 10 in your head.

Exercise your toes by wiggling them for 10 seconds.

Look around the room and describe it in your head as you swallow slowly.

Evoke the image of a place that calms you and visualize it for 10 seconds.

Allow yourself a moment to breathe deeply—in through the nose out through the mouth.

Squeeze the tips of your thumb and forefinger together and release.

Envision a word in your head that relaxes you such as "calm" or "peace."

About the Author

Shyvonne Williams is a professional life-skills trainer committed to a values-driven approach. She devotes much of her motivational work as a group facilitator to working with adults with various barriers. She has researched and authored books covering topics such as leadership, success and self-management and provided "emotional intelligence in the workplace" training for business managers.

In addition to a diverse background in psychology, mediation, life coaching and conflict resolution, Shyvonne holds the following degrees: an Associate of Science from Portland Community College, a Bachelor of Science in Psychology from Portland State University, and a Masters of Art in Psychology from the University of the Rockies. She is currently completing a Doctorate of Philosophy in Organizational Leadership at Grand Canyon University.

Her mission is to motivate others to lead balanced lives by building strong connections and empowering the people they love. "When we learn how to accept those around us," she writes, "we free ourselves to live in harmony."

CMD Group

CMD Group trains clients on the PARTNER Model of interaction. The model is designed to help clients build bridges of connection across differences.

For more information, visit the Web site at www.partner-cmd.com.

Index

AddIQ, 115, 116

Analytical Listening, 62, 175

Articulate, 9, 43, 44, 46, 47, 50, 52, 55, 58, 59, 61, 76, 89, 91, 99, 110, 113, 129, 131, 149, 151, 155, 157, 158, 161, 163, 165, 173, 175, 176, 181

Back-Up Strategy, 131

BIAS, 44, 45, 46, 47, 48, 49, 50, 51, 53, 62, 64, 67, 68, 77, 86, 95, 99, 119, 140, 152, 157, 175, 181

BodyTalk, 28, 30, 31, 32, 33, 38, 47, 81, 157, 159, 175

BOND, 81, 82, 83, 84, 85, 175, 181

Concrete Action Plan, 137

Domino Cycle, 55, 56, 131

EAR, 62, 63, 64, 65, 67, 69, 78, 95, 106, 113, 140, 157, 181

Emanations, 17, 21, 22, 23, 24, 28, 35, 39, 51, 55, 62, 98, 175

Evaluate, 9, 10, 131, 134, 135, 139, 145, 149, 151, 155, 157, 158, 162, 164, 166, 173, 175, 176, 182, 183

EvaluateIQ, 132, 133, 135, 183

Exclusive Listening, 62, 175

IQ (Invitation Question), 175

MindTalk, 35, 36, 37, 38, 43, 55, 62, 124, 157, 159, 175

Next Strategy, 131, 141

Nugget, 9, 10, 113, 114, 117, 118, 119, 120, 121, 124, 129, 131, 132, 134, 136, 149, 151, 155, 157, 158, 161, 163, 165, 173, 175, 176, 182

NuggetIQ, 114, 115

P = P, 50, 52, 53, 175

PICK, 11, 12, 157

Picture, 9, 15, 17, 19, 20, 21, 28, 30, 35, 38, 39, 40, 43, 45, 58, 59, 61, 76, 89, 91, 94, 98, 99, 110, 113, 129, 131, 149, 151, 155, 157, 158, 161, 163, 165, 173, 175, 176

PLUS, 11, 157

Realize, 9, 61, 62, 76, 78, 82, 89, 91, 94, 110, 113, 129, 131, 149, 151, 155, 157, 158, 161, 163, 165, 173, 175, 176, 181, 182

RealizeIQ, 76, 77, 79, 81, 82, 84, 99, 101, 110, 175

Reconstruct, 35, 36, 38, 49, 53, 95, 157

Reinforce, 9, 10, 151, 155, 157, 158, 162, 164, 166, 173, 175, 176, 183

Relational listening, 62, 63

Relational Listening, 175

RELEASE, 32, 37, 82, 131, 157, 159, 176

Shield, 98, 99, 100, 101, 108, 109, 124, 176

SOS Emanation, 21, 22, 23, 98

Span, 167, 173

Take 5, 73

Test, 9, 91, 92, 94, 95, 98, 106, 110, 113, 129, 131, 149, 151, 155, 157, 158, 161, 163, 165, 173, 176

TestIQ, 95, 97, 99, 101, 102, 103, 104, 105, 111

Unmets, 91, 92, 93, 111, 113, 117, 176

Answer Key

Picturing Skill Builder: 10
1. Answer: E....A has blame, B has interpretation, C has assessment, D has selection.
2. Answer: C.... A, B and D have bias.

Articulate Skill Builder: 7
1. Answer: C.   A and B have BIAS.
2. Answer: C.   A and B have BIAS.

Realize Skill Builder: 1
1. Listening Type: **Exclusive**
2. Listening Type: **Analytical**
3. Listening Type: **Relational**
4. Listening Type: **Exclusive**
5. Listening Type: **EAR**
6. Listening Type: **EAR**

Realize Skill Builder: 6
3. Answer: Statement B is the BOND statement...Statement A was not a BOND statement because it had many references to what the other person must do differently; this is displayed by the many "you references," it also states that the other person must change for you to feel cared for.

Statement B: Is assertive and shows that you are taking ownership for your feelings. Talking this way empowers you; it also identifies the behavior that triggered you in a way that does not point finger at the other person. The trigger is factually identified (base) as is your emotional response (offer). This helps to neutralize defensiveness, reduces blame and opens the doors of communication.

REALIZE SKILL BUILDER: 8
Scenario 1: **Answer: A**
Scenario 2: **Answer: C**

TEST SKILL BUILDER: 2
1. Missing: **Agenda**.
2. Missing: **Invitation Question.**
3. Missing: **Agenda and Invitation Question.**

NUGGET SKILL BUILDER: 3
Scenario 1
  1. Directing
  2. Victimizing
Scenario 2
  1. Assuring
  2. Informing
  3. Ordering

NUGGET SKILL BUILDER: 6
1. **Answer: E**....Statement A is Picturing only, B is blaming, , C does not include a review of what occurred, D is only focused on what to do about camping, it's not focused on the unmet, E covers what happened and is a IQ based on the unmet.

EVALUATE SKILL BUILDER: 2
Handle
Handle

Elicitation
Handle
Advantage
Resolve
Resolve
Resolve
Resolve

EVALUATE SKILL BUILDER: 6

1. Answer: C.... A is an example of an EvaluateIQ where the options are lined up with the unmet. B represents a back-up plan.

REINFORCE SKILL BUILDER: 3

1. Answer: C incorporates the PARTNER

CONCLUSION SKILL BUILDER: 2,3,4

Answer: available at www.partner-cmd.com

www.ingramcontent.com/pod-product-compliance
Lightning Source LLC
Chambersburg PA
CBHW060518090426
42735CB00011B/2285